SELLING IS SIMPLE

selling is simple

... if you don't make it complicated

by **KARL BACH**

Founder of San Francisco Life Insurance Company

Advance Books
470 Third Street, Suite 211
San Francisco, CA 94107

Third Edition, October 2001
Fourth Edition, May 2002
© Advance Books

Library of Congress No. 78-72040
ISBN 0-930992-03-2

Publisher:
Advance Books
470 Third Street, Suite 211
San Francisco, CA 94107

TABLE OF CONTENTS

TABLE OF CONTENTS (Continued)

TABLE OF CONTENTS (Continued)

TABLE OF CONTENTS (Continued)

LIST OF ILLUSTRATIONS

Page

FOREWORD TO THE THIRD EDITION

If there ever was a real rags-to-riches story, it is that of Karl Bach. But it isn't just the "ordinary" Horatio Alger story of "poor boy makes good". Karl Bach's life and his accomplishments are lessons and inspirations to all of us. Here is a man who, from the most humble and most unlikely beginnings, made himself one of the most prominent insurance personalities in the United States. The fact that he has amassed great wealth is somewhat incidental. More important are his contributions to the insurance industry, his role as founder of one of California's most important life insurance companies, the contributions that he has made to the art (or is it a science?) of selling, and his many and mostly unheralded philanthropic contributions.

Much to my sorrow and regret, and that of many others, Karl Bach is no longer with us. He has left a rich legacy. This groundbreaking and insightful book is part of it.

It was my pleasure and privilege to have been, for many years, a friend of this outstanding man. I watched, most of the time in amazement, how, without any apparent effort, he built fame and fortune and a prominent insurance company – strictly on the strength of his salesmanship. His performance was prodigious. In the last ten or fifteen years of his life, he never sold less than $20 million worth of life insurance per year. In the last two years of his life, he sold over $40 million and over $50 million, respectively! There are not more than three or four people in the United States who have that kind of a record even today. And Karl was semi-retired at the time! He spent most of his time with his family (he had seven children), playing chess, bicycling, traveling, or attending to one of his many philanthropies.

With a zest for living, with humor and insight, and with unparalleled professional savvy, Karl Bach has revealed all his "selling secrets" in this extraordinary book. Karl Bach spent his selling career in the life insurance business. But the selling techniques, the techniques that made him successful and rich, can be used in any other field of selling. It doesn't make any difference whether it is real estate, machinery, automobiles, books, cosmetics – or life insurance. The techniques to be used, the psychology to be applied to make a customer out of a prospect are pretty much the same. Karl Bach discovered them and he shows us in this book what they are.

And perhaps I am only exaggerating slightly when I say that his philosophy and his techniques can be reduced to only two:

1. Selling is simple – if you don't make it complicated.
2. Don't sell your customers; help them buy!

The 182 pages that follow are really only an elaboration on this theme. Whichever your field of selling, you will greatly profit by reading this book.

Gerard Joffe, President
Advance Books

FOREWORD

I am gratified to write this foreword because the author, Karl Bach, whom I have known personally and professionally for many years, has so much to say that is valuable, practical and applicable. In general, his ideas and techniques help the salesman to think and act with more purpose, spirit and direction. In particular, they sharpen his ability to create situations in which the sale is the inevitable consequence of product insight and "need" realization.

Under Karl's method, the prospect genuinely feels he has bought of his own free will and accord. By the same token, he never suffers those negative and persistently ruinous emotions that tend to predominate when the explanation has been weak or the plan sold inadequate or excessive.

Central to the effectiveness of this book is the fact that Karl actually shows how to build these ideal situations. Methods for transferring the requisite ideas and enthusiasms from the salesman (to whom they are clear, real and immediate) to the prospect (to whom they are frequently a mystery) are set forth in section after section which, taken as a whole, constitute one of the finest selling aids I have ever seen.

The very writing of this book, of course, is a tribute to the unselfishness of this outstanding leader in the field of personal selling. Karl sacrificed many many selling hours to shape his thoughts and experiences into meaningful and cogent language. As a result, he left no stone unturned as he paved the way to success for the typical life insurance salesman.

Through the application of his principles, the reader can most certainly enrich himself as a person and improve his selling ability more than he (or anyone else) would ever imagine.

Joseph E. Boettner, CLU, President
Philadelphia Life Insurance Company

In the following pages you will read about some actual cases as I experienced them over my long career in selling. In order to protect the privacy of the individuals involved, the names and places have been changed. In every other respect, each case is being related exactly as it occurred in practice.

PART I

Selling Is Never Work — It Is Fun

1—Why Read This Book?

Often, when reading a book on selling, I have asked myself why I should have bought it if I knew I would never put the ideas contained in it to work for me. What is the sense of reading further, I ask myself, when I know that I will not change my old habits and when I know that my style of selling is different from that of the writer of this book? I cannot be like him, nor, for that matter, anyone else. What is the sense of reading further when I know that I will not even test the ideas expressed therein?

But I continue anyway. I rationalize: this time is different. This time I promise I will begin to experiment with these new ideas. I promise I will put to work what I feel I can adopt. Perhaps I can improve and do better than I have up to now. I will start right now. I will take pen and paper and I will make some notes. I will mark the book wherever I find an idea that I can use. When I find such an idea and I know this idea is good for me, I will promise to put it into practice. But I know that I will have to be careful that I do not change my own habits in the process. I know I must avoid dropping those ideas which have been successful for me up to this point in time. I will merely blend new ideas into my ever-increasing reservoir of strength in selling.

2—What Makes Salesmen Tick?

You can teach the law; you can teach medicine; you can teach dentistry, engineering and all the other professions. This is how we get good professionals. You can even teach life insurance selling methods and techniques, but you will not necessarily make a good life insurance salesman of your pupil.

A life insurance salesman can have all the knowledge he needs in this business; he may be the best technician; but he will fail, unless he sells. Having been a good life insurance salesman one year is not necessarily going to make one a good salesman in any other year. To grow in life insurance selling, one has to have a steadily increasing sales volume. Standing still is actually going backwards and losing ground.

Prior to starting the San Francisco Life Insurance Company, my experience in helping develop salesmen was very limited. I was invited to speak at various sales meetings of life underwriters, such as conventions and similar gatherings. I would sit up into the middle of the night with my colleagues listening and talking about life insurance selling ideas. I would visit with an endless chain of friends in the business who came to see me with their problems. I would try to answer their questions to the best of my knowledge.

One thing that stood out in my mind was that the men who approached me were never the mediocre salesmen. Why were they always among the leading salesmen in our business? Perhaps this can teach us a valuable lesson. We should never be too proud to ask successful men in our profession for their help and advice. I knew that I needed assistance in many situations. I was never afraid to seek the advice of another colleague.

I could compile here a very impressive list of names of life insurance professionals who have freely helped me over the past years with their advice and their experience. I want to take this opportunity to thank all of them. In a chapter headed, "Men and Mentors," in my book *How I Sell $12,000,000 of Life Insurance Year after Year*, I give credit to these men who have been most helpful to me in my early career. Their names are widely known and respected throughout our industry. Their influence will be with me and will guide me in my entire business life. I regret to have to admit that many times when I needed answers to questions of importance in selling, I could not always obtain them from the management staff of the companies with which I was doing business.

Life insurance selling is not for weaklings. Successful life insurance selling requires character, reliability, strength, conviction, enthusiasm, understanding, responsibility, integrity, love for your fellow men—in short, the qualities of a saint and a fighter. All of these qualities are perhaps in direct proportion to a man's ego.

The successful life insurance salesman also has to possess the listening ability of a psychiatrist, the aggressiveness of a fighter, the ability to recover from a blow (one goes down many times in a row), and the knack of coming back stronger than before. I like to refer to this latter quality as being able to "turn a problem into an opportunity."

These requirements will never change unless people will change and will begin to buy life insurance as they buy groceries. If such a day should come, the complexity of the life insurance business will change with it.

I must confess that I have learned more in the last ten years of my selling career than at any other time. By trying to teach others, I have developed new approaches, new methods, a new sales philosophy and new convictions. I have found myself with less selling-time on my hands, but my desire to keep up my daily objectives of writing one policy and about $1,000 in premiums has never lessened. Somehow I have still found the time to do all the things necessary to build a successful life insurance company.

3—Why I Call Selling A Game

I remember the days when I was working in a big packing house in New York City. I want to stress the word "working." The hours then seemed like days and the minutes seemed like hours. I was continually looking at the clock, waiting for quitting time. There was no question about it: I did not like this type of work. I was not happy. But since I did get paid, I gave it the best I had.

Ever since that time I have been in the game of selling and I have never considered myself at work. I have always considered the business of selling a game and a play. When I made a sale, I won the game. If I did not make the sale, I lost the game. My days in the selling business have always been like minutes for me. Even to this very day, I feel that the time between my arrival in the office in the morning and my departure at night has fairly marched by so fast that I can hardly understand it.

True, there are many days that are disappointing to me because results are poor. But when this happens, I blame only myself. Whenever I fail in making the sale, I play back the action of the interview in my mind and I find the reason for the failure very quickly. In almost all instances I find that it is myself I must blame. I am the one at fault.

After I founded San Francisco Life Insurance Company, many people asked me why I did not become its president. Most people automatically assumed that I would become its

5

president. Consequently, much of my correspondence was addressed to me as president of San Francisco Life. But to me the title of life insurance salesman is about the finest title a man can have. It is also true that a successful life insurance salesman can do better financially than most presidents of life insurance companies. I am appalled when I read an announcement in the insurance journals that says, "Agent Paul Jones has been promoted to assistant manager of his company."

Certainly we do have to have men who are managers. The art of managing is a science all by itself and successful managers are probably even harder to find than successful salesmen. But for me it is not an honor when a salesman is "promoted" from salesman to assistant manager. I believe that there can never be a promotion when you are a good salesman.

Yes, for me, selling is a game. And I am the one who establishes the rules under which I want to play this game of selling. I have found no better rule that could substitute for the golden rule. There is also no substitute for playing the game of selling in the best interests of the prospect.

One situation can be very difficult: you truly love the game of selling but you don't play it often enough. Far too many salesmen have failed in life insurance selling who should have been successful. The cause of their failures was that they did not play the game of selling often enough. If you love the game, don't let your defeats make you take a negative attitude towards the game as a whole. Your mental attitude about your game and how you play it is of utmost importance. Play the game of selling with all your energy and might—by the golden rule and in the interests of the policyholder.

As a life insurance salesman in particular, keep in mind that you are selling a monopoly and that there is *no substitute for life insurance.* I never found a widow who cared what the name of the company was; what type of policy her late husband had purchased; whether the company was a stock company; whether the company was a mutual company. The only thing that this widow cared about was the amount of the check. Yes, there is no such thing as a wrong policy. The only wrong thing about a man dying is "no policy."

It is my sincere belief that all salesmen who are successful sell themselves *more often* on their successes than do the less successful salesmen. The successful salesmen live their business at all times and they live with their business. On my days off I say to myself, "Should I suppress my desire to sell simply because it is my day off, and on my day off I am not supposed to want to work?" But, am I really working when I am selling? The real salesman, in my opinion, is never working, for to him selling is a game. Selling is fun. When you play a game, you are having fun. Are you working? I believe a salesman's attitude on this score determines how successful he will be.

4—Free Energy

Again and again in certain chapters of this book one phrase will be stated repeatedly: *free energy*. This is what I mean by free energy.

When you fill a teakettle full of cold water and put it on a hot stove, there are two ways to describe what happens. You may say that the stove forces heat through the water, or you may say that the water pulls the heat from the stove. For purposes of discussion of salesmanship, I like the idea that the water draws the heat out of the stove. The salesman is the stove; the teakettle is the prospect. The cup of tea that you make with the boiling water is the profit on the sale.

Let's say we have a coal stove. The energy to heat the water has been in the coal millions of years, but it has not been heating anything. You have to set fire to the coal. The fire liberates the energy stored in the coal. The fire sets the energy free so that it can go to work. Isn't it thus with fissionable material? That's the simple principle of free energy salesmanship. You have a hot salesman, a cold prospect and a sale to be made for profit.

Every prospect has built-in resistance which is a form of energy, but this energy can be diverted into other channels and can help make the sale. Free energy salesmanship eliminates the high pressure that is often used by many salesmen. I have been developing my system of free energy salesmanship over many years. You will find many new examples in the pages that follow. I only hope that they will help you understand this simple principle of free energy salesmanship so that you can achieve the results that you desire.

7

5—Thinking Power Or Free Energy—We All Have It!

Most people are not willing to put their brains to work. The ability to think is inherent in all of us, but we have to possess the desire to put this ability to think to work. This ability to think is power that we are storing and if we never use it, it will die with us.

Just as it takes practice for a baby to learn to talk and to use his hands to balance, so too it takes practice to put this ability to think, (which we all have) to work for our own benefit and that of our fellowmen. And since we are in the game of selling, we can make our job so much easier, so much better, if we learn to use the power of our brains. I hope, in the pages following, to translate for you the processes that take place in my mind.

We all know we have certain strengths in our activities. Once we know what they are, we should build on those strengths and not waste our energies on other subjects. We should never be too proud to use tools made available by others in our profession. We should never be too proud to enlist the help of anyone we feel is willing to help. But we should never forget that we should not expect help from anyone. If we do receive help, we should be grateful and do something in return, if we can, for the person who has helped us.

In my selling experience I have found that I spend nearly 80% of my time in getting to the prospect, prospecting and preparing for the interview and only 20% of my time in actual face-to-face communication. It is a simple matter, therefore, to see that if I can get 5% more time in face-to-face interview with the prospect, I can increase my business by 25%. Or, if I can double the face-to-face time with the prospect, I can double my income. Since prospecting takes so much time, it is probably, in the beginning of his career, the single most important function an agent has.

The other day as I talked with a colleague who had attended the Million Dollar Round Table conference, I asked him who had impressed him most of all the men whom he had met at the conference. He told me about a man from the East Coast who had done $400,000 in premiums the previous year, a tremendous accomplishment. I asked him how this agent did it. He told me that all of his business was sold to publicly owned companies. So I said:

8

"How did this agent get to these publicly owned companies?"

I was informed that he was working for a large general insurance brokerage firm whose president was very prominent socially and knew the heads of quite a few large publicly owned Eastern companies. It was he who had opened the doors for this particular life insurance man, enabling him to do such an outstanding job.

It stands to reason, then, that prospecting can be done in various ways and that the proper prestige introduction and connection can be more important than all the knowledge, sales skills and other attributes at one's command. Remember the saying, "It isn't what you know that counts, but whom you know." However, in my personal experience, I have found that I have been able to sell a lot of life insurance by simply calling on people, mostly complete strangers, using the simple method of a direct approach based on the value of my product. Thus I have been able to accomplish the very same thing that a lot of cultivation of the right people—through socializing—entails. This procedure has built connections for me in a natural way, based solely on my own ability and my own personality. But it wasn't the easiest way!

Yes, inherent in every man is his greatest, yet most unused, power—the ability to think. The trouble with most knowledge gathered at sales meetings is the fact that it is put on paper and shelved away. Then we proceed in the same old fashion without ever changing our patterns of operation in the slightest.

Whenever we pick up a sales idea we should make the resolution to review this idea from time to time. We should attempt to use this idea only if it fits into our own personality and sales procedure. It is never wise to stop doing what one has been doing successfully all along, just to replace it with something that we pick up from another salesman. However, we should experiment with every new idea, for what works for one person has been tested and experienced by him, most likely, for a long time. Only gradually will this new idea become part of our own sales procedure and help to improve our own sales operation. So as salesmen, we should continue to experiment at every opportunity, continually perfecting ourselves. Before long the results of our sales procedures will be far beyond anything we ever expected to accomplish.

But what sense is there to study proved sales techniques if one is not determined to make the calls and to approach enough people to put the knowledge to work? It has been my experience that too many salesmen develop sales know-how but never practice their sales skills. This is like a man who studies medicine to become a physician and then makes his living as a pharmacist.

Everybody can study and acquire sales know-how and sales skills and learn sales talks. But no book has yet been written that can teach men to go out and talk to people about life insurance. So, if you are a reader who is not going to put this material to work, I would advise you to stop reading right now and put this book away. You are wasting your time because you do not have the strength it takes to go and see someone about life insurance.

Call reluctance is something that every salesman has to a certain degree. The difference between the mediocre salesman and the outstanding salesman is the number of calls that each one will make. In addition to this difference, however, there is also the difference of a better job of prospecting. A lot of material has been written on this subject. I would recommend that every salesman study and review his methods of prospecting. He should have 100 prospects to call on at all times. However, don't let the fact that you have prospects interfere with your daily habit of getting more. You can never have enough prospects. There will be more on how to find them in another chapter.

You must select and grade your prospects. I personally spend at least one half hour every day in picking the right prospect that I want to call on the following day or the following week. The really successful life insurance salesman has mastered the art of prospecting. He has mastered the art of setting up the worthwhile appointment. He has mastered the art of keeping the prospect's attention during the interview and of creating the desire for his product. And, finally, he has mastered the closing techniques so that he does not lose on the home stretch. He gives it all he has to complete the sale. He has used his brain more often than his feet. It seems that nobody wears out his brain.

6—Your Brain Was Given To You But You Have To Use It For Your Own Benefit

The case of the hitchhiker illustrates the need to use your brain in whatever you do, to think about a problem and to plan its solution properly. So very often I see hitchhikers attempting to thumb a ride, standing in one spot for hours, until someone picks them up. They never really give themselves a chance to be picked up. I see these men and women who are trying to get a ride standing in places so inconvenient or difficult where, even if a driver wanted to pick them up, it would be too dangerous to do so. How much easier it would be for these very same people to consider their objective and pick a corner with a stop sign adjacent where drivers have to stop anyway and where the hitchhiking situation would be a natural event.

I have made this observation so many times that I am truly amazed at people. Why do they not use their God-given brains and put them to work for their own benefit more often and more effectively? It has been stated that most people use only 5% of their capacity for reasoning. Imagine the unused energy and opportunity inherent in all of us!

The reason I bring up the example of the hitchhiker is that it has to do with salesmanship, particularly with free energy salesmanship. So many salesmen do not give themselves a chance to make the sale because they do not think and they do not plan. Unwittingly, they put themselves into the same situation as the hitchhiker who does not plan where to stand, and gives himself thereby a 100 to 1 chance of obtaining a ride instead of perhaps 10 to 1. This can be accomplished simply by using one's God-given power to reason.

7—Who Will Be For Me If I Am Only For Myself?
Thus said Hillel, a great Jewish teacher

In my thinking, hate, jealousy, greed, dishonesty—indeed everything negative—are the greatest enemies of the salesman who wants to excel and succeed. If we can eliminate these negative thoughts that we all have from time to time and improve our habits, we cannot help but improve our results in selling. I know that this is an almost impossible task because at one time or another we all will criticize others' motives; we will criticize people whom we trust; we will gossip about our neighbors; and we will do things that we would prefer not to do if we could but control ourselves more completely.

Realizing that these negative thoughts and negative effects do exist, I have worked on this problem of eradicating them for many, many years. And although I have not been entirely successful no doubt I have improved. The fact that I am aware of this problem often puts me on guard. Quite frequently, I find myself talking about someone to another person and what I am saying is not complimentary. How much nicer it would be if I could find something desirable to say about this individual rather than the negative thoughts I am expressing!

The only person I have ever known who never spoke about another person in a negative fashion was my mother. In looking back at her life, I can truly say that if there ever was a saint, she was one. I cannot remember even one occasion when she spoke in bad terms about another human being. Her life seemed to have been dedicated to doing things for others, to helping the needy and the sick. She would not say much, but you could always see her doing something nice for someone. It seems that every waking moment of her life, she thought of what she could do to make things pleasant for someone else.

If we as salesmen can improve our habits in this direction, we will create in our clients an equal reaction, and a chain reaction can only bring results that favor our objective in making the sale. Naturally, if we do these things only in order to make the sale and that is our sole objective, then we do not really do the nice things that in our hearts, we all want to do. Then the purpose is defeated and the results cannot be the same.

In looking back at many lost sales, I find that the loss of the sale was caused by being sidetracked into discussions that involved my giving unfavorable opinions about other people or unfavorable opinions about other products. It is very easy for one to criticize another. It is very easy for one to see a bad motive in someone else's actions. It is always easy to criticize the other person without knowing the true situation which prompted his action.

I have been working to improve this very, very bad habit—possibly all my life. It has been said that if you do not have something good to say about someone, do not say anything. But it is better still, if you talk about someone, to find his good side to mention. And it is true that every human being has some good side.

This does not mean that one should be unrealistic and not condemn the criminal. But we should not criticize or condemn him until he has been found guilty in a court of law. Even then, we should be cautious in our voiced opinion, because there have been many instances where a jury agreed on the guilt of someone unanimously and the accused later was adjudged innocent.

This chapter should perhaps have been written by a psychologist, who, being well-trained in his field, would have been able to write on this subject in a more dramatic fashion.

St. Francis expressed it best in a prayer:

> Lord, make me an instrument of your peace
> Where there is hatred . . . let me sow love
> Where there is injury . . . pardon
> Where there is doubt . . . faith
> Where there is despair . . . hope
> Where there is darkness . . . light
> Where there is sadness . . . joy.

> O Divine Master, grant that I may not
>   so much seek
> To be consoled . . . as to console
> To be understood . . . as to understand
> To be loved . . . as to love,

>   for

> It is in giving . . . that we receive
> It is in pardoning . . . that we are pardoned
> It is in dying . . . that we are born to eternal life.

8—Good Selling Habits And Getting Properly Prepared

The sales a salesman makes are often made in his mind before he actually makes them. Therefore, there is no substitute for preparation, for conditioning of his mind, in preparing for the sale. Over the years, I have developed some habits which I consider very important in my own method of operation.

One is to spend a few minutes in the evening before going to bed in thinking of what I am going to do the next day and in thinking about the people I want to talk to. The second is to consider what I am going to say and what planning has to be done. I will take a client's file home with me and live with this file quite a while, studying it very carefully. I will develop my plan of action and ask myself how I can improve my prospect's situation when I see him; how I can use as little of his time as possible to obtain the result I want for his benefit. I will make sure that I have all the forms and other tools I might need for the interview.

Further on in this book you will see how I use these forms, most of which I designed for my own personal use. These are simple tools. For the prospect to understand them, they have to be simple. The prospect might not understand anything that is complicated. And this can prevent your sale. Quite often when the prospect does not understand, his pride will not let him tell you that he does not understand. Instead he will state he wants to think about your proposition, and delay does not create sales. Delay is the greatest enemy of all salesmen.

Yes, he will tell you he wants to think about it because he will not confess that, "I don't understand you, Mr. Salesman." Subconciously it would be confessing that he is too stupid to understand. No man will do this. But once he has been confused by you, he will try to seek the answers from someone else. That is how competition frequently enters the picture.

Competition will enter at a time when there was never a thought of competition in the prospect's mind. We, the salesmen, have created our own competition. Doing the right amount of homework and being mentally prepared to see the prospect the next day gives you tremendous power and strength. This power and strength will be with you during the entire sales interview. The fact that you have invested in time for preparation is power and strength in itself.

Why shouldn't the salesman be like the lawyer who prepares himself to go to court? It is hard to imagine an attorney appearing in court, on behalf of his client, completely unprepared. Even with an innocent client he will lose his case. Exactly the same holds true for salesmen who are not prepared. We have to consider a sales interview as important as a lawyer considers a court appearance. We have to prepare. Don't we get paid as much as a lawyer, or even more, when we present our case successfully before our one-man jury, the prospect? Yes, and we don't even have to convince twelve persons, just one.

A sale is a result of so many things we do. Preparation is the beginning of the sale. Lack of preparation is a subconscious desire not to make the sale. Psychologists might call not wanting the sale deeply a desire to punish oneself. So, don't forget. The night before an interview spend the minutes it will take for you to digest and prepare and develop your plan of action for tomorrow. You can never have enough preparation, even if you feel that you don't need it. There is no greater strength for a salesman than to know his product. Yes, you might want to call it homework, if that is what it seems to you. But preparation does not stop here.

Let us imagine that you are about to start on a trip across country in your car. Without thinking very much, you would prepare yourself for such a trip by giving your car a thorough going-over. First of all, you would want to check your gas indicator to see if the tank is full. You would want to check your tires for air and for condition. You would open your trunk to see that the spare is inflated and in good shape. You would check your radiator and you would check your oil. You would make sure your brakes are working properly, and that your windshield is clean. You would give a lot of thought to the problems you could encounter on your journey.

That's what you should do before you see a prospect.

9—Keeping Score With Free Energy

To keep score is a simple way to motivate oneself in a game. Many books have been written on self-motivation. Many more books have been written on the art of selling. But no printed articles and no outstanding books on this subject can create the desire and the determination that is necessary to compete in the game of selling each and every day. This desire and determination has to come from within the salesman himself. To be better than average in selling, one has to love the game. One of the constant self-motivators for me has been my system of keeping score.

It should be natural that every salesman have such a system. In working closely with many salesmen over the last ten years, however, I am amazed that many of them do not know what their score is. How can you play any game without a scoreboard? If we consider selling a business, then we should be like the businessman who at least keeps a daily score of his cash register. I have asked many of these salesmen, "What is your premium income so far this year?" or, "How many lives have you paid for?" And I find they do not have the answer to these (what I consider) vital and important questions.

The scoreboard which I personally keep every day is to me the most important self-motivator that I can have. I have kept this diary continuously for over a quarter of a century. I could not think without it. I would not let a day go by without looking in this book because the progress of my work motivates me to give my very best to this game of selling.

Probably what motivates me the most with my scoreboard is the activity it shows with my clients. The sample scoreboard pages following will show you what I mean. On the left hand of the page I list the applications that are written or the examinations for life insurance that I have arranged. If I don't have at least 20 to 30 in any given month, I know that I am behind and that I am not working at par. Unless there is a payment with the application, it is not important what the amount of the premium is. Therefore, I omit this detail in the written column. When a case is issued and paid for, it then goes on the right side of my page. This is the first time I enter the amount of the premium and the amount of volume.

Although my secretaries keep the same information, this is one part of my operation I personally want to be up to date on at all times. It is from this that I derive the daily strength necessary to continue and to try to out-perform what I have done previously.

This type of motivation has worked for me; it might not work for someone else. I know, however, that most of the men who have started to use my scoreboard after I have properly explained its purpose to them, have benefited from the same motivation that has helped me. I would like to give this tiny bit of advice here: don't start this system unless you have every desire to keep it up. Many salesmen whom I started on this system persevered with it for a while, but then stopped doing it altogether. Fill at least half a page with names of people who are

"SCORE BOOK"

MY DAILY GOAL: One case, $1,000.00 of premium

September

Written Business: Approved Policies:

Name	Examining Physician	Exam- ined	Ap- proved	Ready To Place	Placed
1 Frank Jones	HO	x	x	Henry Luft	x
2 Paul Brown	RE	x	x	Edgar Sayers	
3 H. Motes	HO	x	x	Clyde Jackson	x
4 Syl Beck	Term Conv		x	Dr. Jefferson	
5 Walt Cunningham				Max Snell	
6 Norm Blank	HO	x		Paul Henderson	
7 Jule Hines	RE	x		Dr. Carter	x
.					
.					
40					

(This is the left side of my Score Book)

MY MONTHLY GOAL: $1,000,000, $30,000.00 of premium

September

Paid Business	Amount	Annual Premium
1 Henry Luft	$ 60,000	$1,250.00
2 Dr. Jefferson	100,000	300.00
3 Clyde Jackson	12,500	225.00
4 Dr. Carter	50,000	742.00
.		
.		
.		
.		
40		

(This is the right side of my Score Book)

17

Yearly Summary

This Year: 19				Month	Last Year: 19			
No. of Lives	Volume	Premium	Results: Year to Date		No. of Lives	Volume	Premium	Results: Year to Date
22	$1,805,000	$39,443	$ 1,805,000	January	20	$1,482,000	$28,624	$ 1,482,000
24	1,135,000	20,560	2,940,000	February	24	2,689,500	43,870	4,171,500
8	300,000	8,350	3,240,000	March	21	1,880,000	26,750	6,051,500
20	2,020,000	43,898	5,260,000	April	13	820,000	17,548	6,871,500
14	1,500,000	28,680	6,760,000	May	11	610,000	16,893	7,481,500
14	854,000	17,125	7,614,000	June	21	1,393,000	24,525	8,874,500
27	2,440,000	51,819	10,054,000	July	12	387,000	8,754	9,261,500
12	1,910,000	35,218	11,964,000	August	20	1,262,600	24,840	10,524,100
				September	10	1,595,000	25,060	12,119,100
				October	16	1,625,000	38,580	13,744,100
				November	14	618,000	8,147	14,362,100
				December	16	1,737,500	35,470	16,099,600
				TOTAL:	198	16,099,600	299,061	16,099,600

ready to buy and who have submitted themselves to an examination for life insurance. Regardless of the volume of business, when you have a large number of applications pending, you cannot help but be motivated to be a tremendous success in the life insurance business.

As I look back over a quarter of a century in the life insurance business, I notice that the number of lives that I sell per year is nearly the same now as twenty years ago. The only thing that has changed is the size of the cases. Although I do not write more lives today, I do spend much more time on service work. I now have so many clients to serve that I am prevented from making more calls.

The experience acquired over this period of years, however, has enabled me to do the job of selling more efficiently. It takes me less time now to make a sale and to cultivate clients.

There is one additional aspect which makes my business (or the business of anyone who has stayed in it for a long period of time) so much easier. A large number of sales are made to existing clients and their families.

I'll end this chapter by saying: If you do not intend to keep score, stop selling.

10—Self Organization—Controlling One's Time

Among the many ingredients necessary to become a successful salesman are self-organization and the control of one's time. In working with so many fine and talented salesmen over the years, I have often wondered why some succeeded, some failed and some just withered away.

Many times those who did not succeed had all the requisites to become successful, but they lacked one essential ability: self-organization. I am prompted to write this chapter by a discussion I had recently with one of my old associates—a man of tremendous talent and ability who for years, in spite of my urging, has always been guilty of only mediocre performance.

A year ago I gave him a lead on a prospect who I knew had tremendous potential for him. Six months ago I asked him if he had seen Mr. X. At that point, he had not yet gotten to it. The other day I just happened to remember this lead and again I asked him what had transpired. "Karl, I have to confess, I forgot all about this prospect," he told me. "I know he is an excellent prospect, but I am such a poor organizer of myself. If I could only organize myself properly I would really be in the big leagues."

I knew this statement was true and right then it occurred to me to say a few words in this book about self-control and organization of time.

What should my associate have done when I gave him this lead? In order to self-organize, you need a self-organizer. And you need first of all the desire to follow the direction of your self-organizer.

My self-organizer is my little appointment book, an annual diary which I keep in my shirt pocket at all times. In it I write down the names of the people I want to see in a particular week. As I contact them, I check their names off my list. Any name that is not checked off is carried forward to another week. Sometimes I do not check off a name immediately, but as I continuously review the pages, I carry forward this name to a future possible time when I can see this prospect.

Thus I always have this name in front of me and I know that I have to make the call. Since I know that every call is worth a certain amount of money, and since once I have made a call I have an investment of my time which I will not let go wasted, I am constantly before people. And because of that, there is continuous activity which keeps me in a positive frame of mind. This constant knowledge that I have another name to call keeps my spirit up and my enthusiasm great so that I can inspire the people to whom I talk and can motivate them with the power of free energy.

A good example of self-organization is found in chapter 36: If You Love To Play Your Game, Why Not Do It Every Day? There have been many books written on this subject and, as I do not want to belabor a subject which others have written about more eloquently than I ever can. I merely want to point out here that determination to follow through on a given course is the KEY factor in self-organization. The desire to do the job, the determination to eliminate non-essentials, to write out a course of action and to stick with it at all times, come what may, is a tough proposition. However if you were the pilot of a plane, that is exactly what you would have to do. And you are the pilot of your own ship to success in selling. If you do as the pilot of the plane, you will get to your destination.

11—Ten Self Motivators

1. I'm not only a salesman. Even more I am a businessman. My time is my stock-in-trade. When I waste my time, I am wasting my money. I'm running a business as much as if I were running a store. For me, not to employ my time intelligently is like closing the store during business hours.
2. Remembering that I am a businessman first and a salesman second, I take the long-range point of view. I do not kid myself and I do first things first.
3. I'm going to make a number of intelligent calls daily that a good businessman would make. I know that I cannot fool the law of averages. If I make only half the calls that I should, I know that I will eventually be doing only half the business that I should.
4. I will keep score because selling is more enjoyable if I make it a game. I will set myself a quota by which to judge my efforts. When I am behind in my quota I will work like hell and worry like hell. When I am ahead of my quota I will only work like hell.
5. The call that didn't bring a sale brings me closer to the call that will. The law of averages works such that the man who gets more no's will also be the man who gets more yes's.
6. I avoid unnecessary worry and tension by watching my personal finances carefully and not spending money I cannot afford to spend. Any damn fool can spend money. It takes a smart man not to.
7. Simplicity will help increase my percentage of yes's. I will try to keep things as simple as possible. I will do first things first. During working hours I will solicit.
8. Everyone else has butterflies in his stomach. Why should I be different? However, there is no law against making calls. Seeing people will result in interviews.
9. It takes courage to make calls. Moreover, if it didn't the insurance companies would simply hire ribbon clerks for a low salary.
10. I have a main track to travel on. I will pick out a plan that I am particularly sold on. My enthusiasm will make me more effective.

12—Why A Salesman Should Be A Good Businessman

In my experience with salesmen, I have found that a great number—even among the very successful—are very bad businessmen when it is a question of their own personal finances. It is my own recommendation that every salesman develop the habit of being a good businessman in his own personal life and his own affairs. I believe that the time and study required to develop this important habit is the best investment that a salesman can make.

Many of the salesmen I know are deeply in debt and are continually pressured by their bills and obligations. Personally, I feel that this pressure can be detrimental to their sales efforts. There are two schools of thought among sales managers: one is that because the salesman has to meet his bills, he will work that much harder. The other school of thought is that if the salesman is sound financially, he can direct all his efforts to his job completely without the pressure of his personal finances and he can do a better job for his prospect.

I am a believer in the latter school of thought. I am a strong believer that the sounder the salesman's own personal finances are, the better the job he will do for everyone concerned. Not having the pressure of worrying about how and when to meet financial obligations, he is able to dedicate his energy toward more sales and toward improving his own operation. It is for that reason that I would like to recommend to those who have personal financial problems to take a course in business and financial management or find material to study that will help improve business habits so as to achieve financial security. With a sound financial foundation, salesmen will have the strength and power to use free energy salesmanship more often and more effectively.

Through what you will learn about business and business habits you will come to better understand your prospect's business. You will see his business from a viewpoint which is different from his. And you will be better able to make recommendations and suggestions that can help him.

Naturally, you have to be very careful whenever you volunteer recommendations of any kind. I am thinking here of a pediatrician, a client of mine. This man had a thriving practice, but whenever we discussed his financial situation I found that he was always short of money; and when he finally told me his income, I was amazed that it was so low. I knew that his income was not in line with the income of other pediatricians who did not have as large a practice. This doctor was very competent and extremely dedicated.

I asked him about his fees: what he was charging for an office call; what he was charging for a house call. When I compared these figures with what I had been paying my own pediatrician, I was amazed at the tremendous difference. He was simply not charging enough. I mentioned this fact to him and the next time I visited with him, he thanked me for having brought this to his attention. He increased his charges. He found no objection from his patients to this increase and, as a result, he was able to afford a much larger life insurance policy than I thought he could purchase. We have since become very good friends and I have helped him with other business advice.

In many instances, it is advisable to recommend that a specialist be called in to make an analysis of the client's business affairs, with the objective in mind to improve the operation by either reducing expenses or increasing income, or a combination of the two. The medical profession has specialists who are very competent in this field. And so has practically every other business.

It is wise for you to know who these specialists are because they can also recommend you when the question of insurance arises. If you have financial problems or if your business is not operating as efficiently as it could be, it could also be good advise that you yourself call in a specialist. Many times your CPA will do, as it is much easier for an outsider to find room for improvement than for you to do the same thing. Just as a doctor who becomes ill can always call in another doctor to treat him, so should the businessman who runs into trouble.

To the young salesman I would like to give this bit of advice: the habits you acquire in your early career will be with you for a long time. Start with good habits. Start with a desire to be financially sound and your success in any chosen field will be easier to obtain.

With all the problems that life has in store for us and all the opportunities that these problems bring with them, if we can avoid the unnecessary worries and risks we have easier sailing. In spite of all the modern equipment in our aircraft industry, there are still days when planes cannot leave the ground. There are certain risks that one should not take.

Most people like to live beyond their means. I always have believed that it is a good thing (and it will never hurt) to live a little lower than your means. That extra margin of safety can never hurt. It is always easier to increase one's standard of living than to decrease it. Since we are living in a money economy, it is wise to play the economic game as intelligently as possible. And if we do, we cannot help being financial successes.

13—Unless You Prospect, You Can't Find Gold

1. In selling it all starts with a name.

2. A name becomes a prospect.

3. A prospect means nothing unless he becomes a client.

4. A client is the source of more prospects, a source of the best prospects.

5. If you don't talk to prospects first, they won't talk to you.

6. Prospects do not bite.

7. There is no *cold* canvass—when you see living people.

8. The call you make where you didn't sell will bring you closer to the call on which you will sell.

9. A barrier is overcome but not by ducking it.

Among sales managers it is often said that a salesman's biggest problem is prospecting. To this I cannot agree. Since the world is full of people and people as a rule are friendly, there should never be a problem with prospecting. In my opinion, the real problem is to overcome the inborn barrier that most of us have to make the first step towards the prospect. Perhaps we feel that we do not want to be rejected, and by not making the call we avoid this disappointment.

There is no sense in studying the methods of prospecting if we are not first willing to make up our mind to eliminate this barrier towards the prospect. We have to remember that people do not bite. We have to remember that every product in the world has to be sold. And anything that has to be sold requires the services of the salesman. We have to remember that every man is a salesman and everyone is selling something to somebody.

In the following pages, I am showing you the places from which I get my prospects. Today, after many years of prospecting, all of this has become a daily habit. When I read the newspaper in the morning, I am prospecting. When I am driving to work in my car, I am prospecting. When I am riding the commuter train, I am prospecting. When I go shopping with my family, I am prospecting. When I attend a school meeting for my children, I am prospecting. I am prospecting wherever there are people. I am prospecting wherever there are names in the news, because people are our business.

However, the key to good prospecting is to pick the prospect that fits your personality. Pick the prospect with whom you feel comfortable. You don't know this until you have met him. But with much practice, you can ascertain in advance—either in your telephone call before setting up the appointment, or, if it is a referred lead, by what you are told about the prospect—if he will be an outstanding lead for you or only a poor one.

A regular part of my daily procedure before calling on a new prospect is to pick out the prospect whom I consider the very best. There is an important reason for this selection. By picking the best prospect first, my chances of getting results are greater. When you get poor results, you feel unhappy and that feeling reflects itself in the next call. When you obtain good results, you feel happy; and once you are in a happy mood, you will make your prospect happy. You are creating a chain reaction which reflects itself in your prospect. He will be energized by your cheerful attitude. Your natural smile will be like a laser beam of energy that is working for you. By avoiding unnecessary obstacles in selection of your prospects, you pave the path for more sales.

Therefore, it is often better to spend a little more time in going through your prospects, and mentally grade them, than to make a call irrespective of priority in the hope that the law of averages will take care of you. There is no law against improving on the law of averages. There is no question in my mind that a salesman, by merely picking at random any number of people and by using a simple and sound approach continually, cannot help but become successful. However, the real salesman who wants to develop his salesmanship into a fine art will use everything in his power to get better results along the road.

It all starts with having a prospect. Without a prospect, a sale could never be made. Therefore, the study of the art of prospecting should be never-ending for the salesman who wants to go places.

I do not mean to suggest, however, that one should call only the big prospects and neglect the little ones. I would rather like to suggest that one should call on people who have potential to grow in their own field, people with whom we can grow; and that the emphasis at all times should be on opening as many accounts as possible.

PART II

Selling Is Simple . . . If You Don't Make It Complicated

14—On Prospecting

In the daily newspaper there lies an unlimited number of possible prospects for the salesman. Regardless of the methods a salesman uses to get to see a prospect, if he uses these methods often, he will gradually refine them and improve on them. I could continue this subject of prospecting here and write a book filling a large volume. Perhaps I will do so in the future. However, all your prospecting is worthless unless you make the personal calls. Make the calls, and the more calls you make, the better the results will be. Whatever techniques are employed, there is no substitute for making the call.

The businessman must respect the salesman who wants to make a living, because all businesses are selling something and have salesmen in the field. When this is recognized, then the right to be called a salesman is won.

One very important thing: Whenever you have a prospect secured through a newspaper column, go to work on him immediately. Do not let the name cool off. While you are hot, while you believe you have a prospect, that is the time to act. Go to work on him at once and you will find that the results you will achieve will be way above the average. If you keep a name in your files, it will suddenly lose its importance; it will lose its value to you; and nothing will have been accomplished.

New Incorporations

Corporations, especially new ones, are the sources of lots of business. There are several ways to find out if you have a good prospect by just reading what appears under "New Incorporations" in your local papers. (See the following illustration) First notice the amount of capitalization, indicating whether you are dealing with a small or a large business. Then notice the attorneys who have incorporated the business. You have a better chance to do business if this happens to be a law firm that knows you. Often, If I know a lawyer very well, I will call him and ask him about the prospect, and frequently he will volunteer to give me an introduction.

The names of the people who are incorporating are your key prospects. The newspaper article tells you where they live, what types of prospects you may expect to encounter and the type of business. You might seek to get an introduction to these prospects from one of your present clients who is in a similar business. Keep in mind that people in similar professions or businesses usually know each other.

New Incorporations
(By County)

Landmark Construction Co. ($20,000-$10 par), Santa Clara (building construction). Ware & Freidenrich, 2600 El Camino Real, Palo Alto, Dirs.: David Freidenrich, 20 Willow Rd., Apt. 28, John Freidenrich, 935 San Mateo Dr., Menlo Park; Marcella T. Yano, 311 Bryant St., Palo Alto.

Par-Pak Corporation (20,000 shares-no par), San Joaquin (sale of farm products). Chickering & Gregory, 111 Sutter St., S.F. Dirs.: John Philip Coghlan, Leslie P. Jay, F.S. Bayley, 111 Sutter St. S.F.

Birth Notices

For many years I have followed the birth notices in the daily newspaper. Many of my valuable clients have come from these birth notices. In the early years of my career, I indiscriminately called on anybody and everybody. In later years, I became more selective. I picked the better neighborhoods, indicated by the address, or I picked the type of prospect with whom I felt I wanted to work. Professional men were my best prospects. Usually if a doctor or a dentist has an addition to the family, the birth notice will say "Dr. Jones," instead of "Mr. Jones." I have done extremely well over the years with these prospects.

By looking through these notices daily, I was also on top of any new additions to the families of my present clients before some other insurance man was able to take over.

In Chapter 15, "The Telephone Wire—Your Best Connection," I give you the approach I was using successfully for a long period of time.

VITAL STATISTICS
Births

COWDREY—To the wife of Robert Cowdrey, 3125 Turk St., on March 29, a daughter.

GOLDBERG—To the wife of Jerry Goldberg, 769 Francisco St., on March 28, a daughter.

SCHOLNICK—To the wife of Dr. Perry L. Scholnick, 3720 Anza St., on April 10, a son.

Deaths

BLUMBERG, CHARLES B., on April 8, father of Gertrude Resnick, Esther Jacobs and Sadelle and Albert Blumberg. Services at Sinai Memorial Chapel. Interment, Eternal Home.

BRENNER, VLADIMIR, on April 9, husband of Seraphima Brenner. Services at Sinai Memorial Chapel. Interment, Eternal Home.

Death Notices

By reading the daily death notices, I not only kept myself informed about my own clients, but also I could tell if some friend or relative of my clients had passed away. This would always be another reason to call on that client to review his insurance program. He had looked death in the face, so to speak, and had seen some of the problems that death can create. Also, I make prospect cards on all the relatives of the deceased. Often I would remember the name of someone related to the deceased whom I had called on in the past but did not sell. I usually found him a better prospect because of this unfortunate event in the family. Also, by reading who attended the funeral and who were the pallbearers, I had a new cycle of prospects who were perhaps a little more motivated by the part life insurance plays in life for the living.

The age of the person who passed away is an important clue. After a man dies, people who were associated with him will be more conscious of life insurance—all the more so if they are young. Here is a good procedure: Say Mr. Jack Smith, age 42, Sales Manager of the XYZ Company, died. If you are now calling on the XYZ Company, you will ask for the deceased. You will be referred to the New Sales Manager. The man who died is a good talking point to get the subject of life insurance going.

It isn't exactly pleasant that we have to use methods of this kind to get prospects; however, I feel that there has never been a "wrong" way to sell life insurance, if the desire is to help. Also, I know there is no "wrong" company and I know there is no "wrong" policy. When a man dies, there is usually never enough life insurance.

Newspaper Items On Promotions And Appointments To Executive Positions

These men whose names and pictures appear are always good prospects. Their pictures give you an idea of their approximate ages, which are always important to note. You can tell by the kinds of jobs to which they have been promoted what their incomes might be. You will know that a promotion is usually accompanied by an increase in salary, which makes the man a better prospect. And there will be another prospect waiting for you: the man who took his former job. He also has been promoted and you can get a reference to that man from the man you are going to call on, if you have sold yourself to him first.

We process this type of prospect in this fashion: my secretary will place the clipping of this news item on my letterhead and send it to the prospect with the following remarks: "Congratulations! More power to you. I will be in touch with you soon with a brand new idea. Signed, Karl Bach." I can assure you that whoever receives this on my letterhead will remember me because I have remembered him.

Businessmen

IN THE NEWS

Harold W. Alexander has joined the Folsom-based Flomatics Division of Crane Co. as controller. He leaves a similar position with Koehring Co.'s Ko-Cal Division to join Crane.

The Northern California Industrial Relations Council has elected **D.M. Holley** of the Bancroft-Whitney Co. vice president; **M. Hugh Foskett**, IBM Corp; secretary; and **John G. Bradley**, Kaiser Aluminum and Chemical Corp., treasurer.

Prospectus

The "bigger" prospect can be found by studying the prospectus of a company that is about to go public or has just gone public. Many times the big prospect is a selling stockholder and the prospectus tells you the amount of shares owned by the selling stockholder and his family. By multiplying the number of shares by the amount of money he will receive, you have a good idea of the worth of this man's holdings in the company—a good indication of the type of prospect awaiting you. You also know that he will have cash to pay his premiums. This type of man is very receptive to new ideas if you can make yourself interesting enough to talk to him.

The prospectus tells you a variety of other things: the officers of the company; their salaries; their shareholdings. You can figure the value of their holdings by multiplying the number of shares by the sales price of the stock. The prospectus also tells you the value of the stock options and retirement plan and whether the company has a deferred compensation plan. The prospectus gives you an operating statement and balance sheets, etc.—everything you need to know to find a reason for life insurance. What follows will illustrate what I mean.

The Company's business is also subject to factors which adversely affect the total housing market, such as the availability and terms of financing to dealers and retail purchasers and . . .

Employees

On December 31, 19 , the Company had 270 employees, of whom 230 were in production, 21 in supervision and engineering, 8 in sales and 11 in office and administration. Employees are provided with paid annual vacations, group life insurance and medical and hospitalization benefits. The employees of the Company are not covered by collective bargaining agreements, and the Company has never experienced a strike or work slowdown because of labor relations problems. Management considers employee relations to be excellent.

Properties

The Company's executive offices and plant for the production of _____ models are located in _____California on a 6.7 acre site. These facilities include a 77,000 square foot building constructed by an independent developer in 19 in accordance with the Company's specifications. The land and building are leased at a monthly rental of $6,062 (plus taxes and . . .

Officers and Directors

The executive officers and directors of the Company are as follows:

Name	Office
_____	Chairman of the Board and President
_____	Vice President, Treasurer and Director

_____ founded the Company and has been chairman of the Board and President since its inception. Mr._____ has been engaged in the mobile home industry since 1940, having . . .

Remuneration

The aggregate remuneration paid by the Company during the fiscal year ending May 31, 19 , to each director and to each of the officers of the Company whose aggregate remuneration exceeded $30,000 that year, and the aggregate remuneration paid to all directors and officers of the Company as a group during the year, are as follows:

Stock Options

On December 19, 19 , the Company adopted a qualified stock option incentive plan (the . . .

Certain Transactions

Mr._____ died in November, 19 , and on October 31, 19 the Company entered into a contract with his estate for the purchase of his 353,571 shares for an aggregate purchase price of $96,298. The final installment . . .

1. WHY and HOW did I pick this prospect?

2. WHEN shall I make my call?

3. WHAT shall I do before the call?

4. WHAT will I say when I call?

5. WHAT will I show him and WHY?

6. WHEN is the best time to see him?

7. WHAT is the best way to get there?

8. Do I have all my tools in my briefcase—what tools do I need for this interview?

15—The Telephone Wire—Your Best Connection

I remember my early days of selling when I tried to learn to use the telephone. It was awfully hard for me to talk to a stranger on the phone. It required all the energy at my command. It was tough for me to overcome the barrier created by the distance. I will never forget how often I broke out in a deep sweat while using the telephone. Usually after I finished my call, I was wringing wet. I used to shy away from using the phone. I would rather have made ten calls in person to find one prospect in than to make one phone call. In making these direct calls, I acquired the skill that it takes to open up with people whom I had never met before. This was one way for me to create the personal connection needed to make a sale. I will never forget that in many an instance, having made this cold call, I would not sell the man I intended to see but instead would meet someone else I would sell. This was entirely unexpected.

I often wondered if I wasn't just plain lucky. I usually opened up with an interest getting idea. Then I tried to make an appointment with the prospect for that very same moment, or, if he could not grant me the time I made a date for some time later on.

In those days, my sales know-how was very limited. I had received very little sales training. As time went on, I continued to use the telephone off and on. Finally I acquired the steady habit of using it before calling on a prospect. I found that I could cover a wide breadth of territory in a much shorter period of time. I would save a vast amount of traveling time, but most of all a lot of time waiting in offices. (How could this waiting time be helped when I had made the call without a previous appointment?)

I can truly say that the telephone wires are my best connections. Without a telephone today I would be lost. I received most of my practice in the use of the telephone in the days when I used as prospects young couples whose names I found in the birth notices columns in the daily newspapers. You might be interested in the approach I used at that time.

I always phoned these young couples anywhere from three to six months after their baby was born. I picked out neighborhoods in the city whose addresses indicated the income bracket of those persons with whom I felt most comfortable at that time. I also tried to select persons who lived close to my own home, because most of my interviews resulting from these telephone calls were made in the evening.

I would use the following approach:

"Mrs. Jones, this is Karl Bach speaking. I am making a life insurance survey. I am quite sure that you have been approached since your baby was born by many insurance companies. Isn't that correct? What has your decision been regarding life insurance? What has your reaction been regarding life insurance?"

Then I would let the woman or the man (usually it was the wife who answered the phone) do the talking.

Then I would say: "How is the baby? How many do you have?" And again I would let the mother talk about her child. My next question would be: "When will you be interested in purchasing life insurance either for yourself or for the education of the baby?"

This sales talk was very effective. If I spent three hours on the telephone (which is a very, very tough job) I would always find one or two prospects who purchased life insurance from me. Later on, I refined this method by asking the wife, if she answered the phone, if her husband was in, and if he was not in, I would ask:

"Can you give me a phone number where I can reach him? This is Karl Bach calling."

In most instances, the wife would be happy to give me the name and telephone number of the husband's place of business. I would then inquire about the baby and, although this woman had never met me, she would volunteer all kinds of information that was very helpful when I contacted the husband later.

I would then use this telephone number to call the husband at work and make an appointment to see him during lunchtime or business time, if permissible. In the earlier period of my sales development, I would simply call at the business and ask for the husband. If he was not in, I would ask for the owner of the establishment—to get value from this call so that it was not wasted. By following this simple system during the early building of my career, I was able, week after week, year after year, to get my sale for the day.

It is for that reason that I challenge every salesman in the life insurance business to make at least one sale a day, because it is that easy. (More on this thought later). All that is required is the determination to see the people and the willingness to tell your story with conviction, with enthusiasm and with the desire to be of help.

16—A Silent Way To Sell Yourself

Whenever I am mailing something to a client pertaining to a new purchase, or before making a call, I use a third party influence. Every mailing piece that leaves my office includes some prestige bulletin designed to build me up in the eyes of the prospect. It cannot be said too often that the agent has to sell himself before he can sell his product. And, in order to sell himself, he has to use every possible means at his disposal. One of the most effective devices for prestige building is the so-called prestige bulletin.

I am showing a few here that I have been using successfully over the years.

Anything I can do to keep my name before the public (in a favorable light) helps in making my sales easier. I am convinced

WE PAY TRIBUTE TO

KARL BACH

1970 Production: **$25,000,000**

A mark of achievement in the Life Insurance Industry is when a salesman sells $1,000,000 of Life Insurance in one year. It is the direct result of a salesman's skill and experience, coupled with his desire to provide outstanding service to his clients . . . KARL BACH'S slogan is: "'I don't sell insurance. I help you buy it.''

★ ★ ★ ★ ★ ★ ★

During 1970, KARL BACH helped his friends and clients buy $25,000,000 of new life insurance. This achievement distinguished him not only as the foremost salesman of SAN FRANCISCO LIFE INSURANCE COMPANY, but as one of the Nation's outstanding Life Insurance specialists. The plans and technical assistance which MR. BACH needed to meet the needs and demands of his clients were provided by

Author-Lecturer
Salesman Extraordinary

SAN FRANCISCO LIFE INSURANCE COMPANY
Affiliate of Tenneco, Inc. and The Philadelphia Life Companies
160 Sansome Street, San Francisco, California 94104

37

of any life insurance company, yet his compensation does not rank with that of modern business executives.

I am referring here to benefits such as split-dollar life insurance, deferred compensation, etc. Through my experience in working with virtually hundreds of agents I found that they don't think in terms of net profit. Instead, they think in terms of volume of business and frequently completely overlook the fact that volume of premiums is more important than anything else.

During the last three years I have conducted throughout California a monthly sales meeting entitled, "The Free Energy Sales Forum." At these forums we have covered every aspect of the life insurance business. Those attending these meetings were surveyed to determine how many of them had invested money in their own industry. I was amazed to discover that only a small percentage owned common stock in any life insurance company.

Growth Stocks—Most life underwriters, I'm sure, are familiar with the tremendous growth that has taken place in life insurance stocks during the last 25 years. For example, I entered the life insurance business in 1943. If every year since 1943 I had invested $500 in the common stock of an eastern company located in the same city as the company with which I spent most of my life insurance career, my total investment would have amounted to $10,500.

This investment of $10,500 would have grown to be worth in excess of $600,000 today. This example is not an isolated one. It has been true for many stock life insurance companies in the United States. Isn't it shocking to learn that so many of the men who made this tremendous growth possible are not participating in the financial rewards of their own labor?

I would like to acknowledge my gratitude to one of my colleagues who aroused my interest in the investment possibilities of our own industry early in my career. He gave me this advice: "The life insurance salesman who himself is financially sound and strong will be best able to advise his clients with sound financial planning. Being successful himself, successful business men will seek his advice."

One of the nation's outstanding personal producers, Karl Bach has also made his mark as an author and as president and founder of San Francisco Life. His book, "How I Sell $12 Million of Life Insurance Year After Year," was published by Pacific Books in 1960. A native of Germany, he immigrated to the U. S. in the middle of the Great Depression, entered selling as a Fuller Brush man. His address: San Francisco Life, 25 Kearny St. at Maiden Lane, San Francisco 8.

The Survivors—It is my strong belief that the life insurance man who wants to be a successful businessman is the one who will survive best in our business. I know the problems facing our industry in obtaining good salesmen. I'm familiar with the aptitude tests and recruiting methods. I'm also aware of the various financing methods used by companies to bring men into our business.

I believe, however, that a new approach in recruiting would be in order. If we consider life insurance selling a profession and an outstanding career, why should it not be like going into the law, dental, or medical profession? If my son wanted to become an attorney, he would first have to go to law school, pass his bar examination, lease an office, buy the necessary furniture and equipment, and wait for his clients to come. After a considerable lapse of time, he would be able to get back his investment. It would take even longer before he could take home a profit.

The life insurance salesman who is on commission only can be earning money right away. But if he is truly a professional underwriter, he should

SECURITY

FOR

SALESMEN

by KARL BACH

want to invest in the equities of his business with his own funds. He should become a success not only in life insurance salesmanship, but also in his own personal financial affairs. He will then be able to advise his clients for their benefit first, because he will be free of personal financial pressures and worries. ■

38

that an entire book could be written on this one subject only: how to build prestige. But that is the job of a public relations man. For that reason, it might be wise for you to employ the services of a good public relations man. Remember, you have to sell yourself, if someone else sells you first, it is even better. A written article about yourself is excellent, for example. When the client sees you later, he will recall that he read about you. You will have built a favorable image of yourself, which cannot help but influence his final decision.

Wouldn't it be wonderful if we could work like the merchant who sits in his store and waits for the customers to come in? All we would have to do is write up the order. But every merchandiser, because he is faced with fierce competition, has to advertise continually to influence the public to come to see him.

The commodity we sell, life insurance, is one that is bought because of the purchaser's love for someone else. But because it is an intangible product, the buyer feels that he can always get it at a later date. He needs the guidance of a real salesman.

17—Before The Interview

A.   Questions Before The Interview

1.   Who is my prospect? What do I know about him? Who can tell me more about him? Who are his friends? What about his family, his interests, his attitudes, his personality, his character, his relationship to others?

2.   Why am I the insurance man who can best serve my prospect? Can I put myself in his position and think as he does? Why is my product or service particularly well-suited to my prospect?

3.   What ideas do I have that will be of value to my prospect? Am I prepared to present alternatives for the solution of his problems?

4.   Is his need for insurance in connection with his business enterprise or his personal financial situation, or both?

What products can I offer that will fit his financial position today and in the future? What service does my prospect require, and am I prepared to render this service?

5. Where shall I see my prospect? Where will the conditions of an interview provide maximum opportunity to make and close the sale? Will interruptions be present? Shall I see him at his home, his place of business, at a luncheon or dinner, at his club or mine, in the office of his attorney, accountant, or that of an interested third party?

6. When is the best time to see my prospect? Would a breakfast appointment before his work day begins be best? Is the morning the time during which he is least busy? Is he relaxed after 4:00 in the evening? Is Saturday, or perhaps even Sunday, the best time to get his undivided attention? Maybe a rainy day or a weekend will find my prospect at home wanting to discuss his problems.

7. When will he be in the best mood to accept my ideas? Is today the best time to see him, or is he likely to be more receptive after the holidays, after tax time, as soon as he returns from a vacation? Timing is vital.

8. What one prize idea is likely to wipe out all obstacles so that the sale can be closed? What is my real "Dynamite" punch? What idea will have the strongest impact with my client? What makes his problems and his needs change into his wants? How do I best coordinate the who, the why, the what, the when and the WOW, in order to get my prospect to buy?

B. Positive Thoughts That Flash Through My Mind Before Each Interview

Before every interview there are many thoughts that flash through my mind. What is my objective for the interview? How much time do I have? How much time will my client give me? How long will he be attentive to my proposition? I have always to remember that there is only a limited amount of time during which a prospect will be tuned into my proposition. When that time is up I know from experience that whatever I say from there on will be wasted, because my prospect does not listen with both ears.

I decide before every interview that my objective is to make one sale consisting of several small sales. Each small sale has to stand on its own feet. The first sale that I have to make is myself. My prospect has to be sold on me—that I am the right man with whom to do business. The second sale that I have to make is to get my prospect to see in his own mind that life insurance is the one thing that can give him the peace of mind and the happiness he needs to go about his daily work. The third sale I have to make is to get the prospect to submit himself to a medical examination. I will never be able to help him buy life insurance unless I can sell him first to the insurance company. These are my minimum objectives. I must make these sales in order to be able to make the final sale.

I will go one step further if I can. If I can get an agreement on these little points, I will immediately ask for a check for all or some part of the premium so that my prospect's family is covered during the time it takes the insurance company to underwrite the risk.

It is very essential to take time to go through these steps before each and every interview. But regardless of what strategy I am using, I must never forget that I have to be flexible and willing to make a change in my formula if the situation so indicates. In my book, *How I Sell $12,000,000 of Life Insurance Year after Year*, I have devoted a chapter to explaining the formula "1 + 1 = 1." (See Appendix for an excerpt from that chapter.) This formula, if properly used, cannot help but bring every salesman to greater heights in sales, provided he is willing to pay the price of his time and determination.

C. Negative Thoughts That Flash Through My Mind Before The Interview

There are some thoughts we all have but would rather not admit to. We do not like to admit that it takes guts to call on strangers, but in order to be successful in selling we have to overcome call reluctance.

What are these negative thoughts we all have?

What is the sense of my calling on Mr. Jones, President of the XYZ Manufacturing Company? He doesn't know me.

He has never heard about me, so why should he talk to me?

He probably buys his insurance from someone that he is close to socially, or he has a relative in the business.

He will never buy from me.

Why should I call on Dr. Smith? He is so busy that he will never have time to see me.

What have I got that will make him interested in buying from me even if I get an appointment?

There is no doubt in my mind that calling on him is a waste of time.

I am not his equal and I will never get to first base.

But when these negative thoughts flash through my mind I brace myself and say, "no, on the contrary, I am the best man he can get. I am going to give him the very best I have. I will be better than anyone else he could get."

It is important to get rid of all negative thoughts before the interview. Review them in your mind and then discard them and replace them with positive thoughts. And sell!!

D. Preparation Just Before The Interview

You are only a few minutes away from your next interview. Take time again to think about the prospect's problem and review what you have already done. Take time to prepare again and to think and to sharpen your wits. Again make sure all your tools are ready and handy. Set the stage properly. Have your plan of action developed in your mind. Do not leave anything to chance. Keep firmly established in your mind that you want to make that sale today, not tomorrow. Yes, today. Sell yourself on this idea.

And then you will bubble with energy. And this energy will radiate to your prospect and he will buy from you. After he has bought from you, you feel that you have won a victory because you have made your sale. You have won in the game called selling. And when you win you are happy. When you are happy, you radiate happiness and you make the people around you happy. When you make people happy, they in turn will make you happy. Thus you have created a cycle of happiness. The man who has bought from you will like you. The man you did not sell, as a general rule, will not like you. Therefore, isn't it wonderful to have as many people as possible like you?

The man who has bought from you will never tell his friends that he has been sold by you. On the contrary, he will tell his friends that he has just given you some business. Yes, he will never say that anyone has sold him. But do you really care what he says, as long as he has bought from you? The only thing that really matters is that your game of selling is successful. And with it will come all the financial reward that is so important in our modern society.

Now, with this mental conditioning you are ready to face the prospect. You are ready now to convince him that to act today and not to delay is in his best interest.

18—The First Minute With Your Prospect

It has been said by many students of salesmanship that the first minute or two is the most important time you will spend with your prospect. The impression formed of you in the prospect's mind during this time can very well be the deciding factor when it comes down to the decision of the prospect as to who it is who will do business with him. It stands to reason, then, that before every sales presentation, a salesman should give this first minute or two a great deal of thought, and he should know exactly what he is going to do in these opening moments.

For one thing, let the prospect feel that you are a person who can do him good. This is best done with a powerful opening statement which arouses a desire on the part of your prospect to get to know what you already know. You have to appear to your prospect as the man who deserves his confidence and as the man with whom he can feel comfortable. This is where proper grooming comes in, but we shall not cover that subject here.

It never hurts in the very beginning of a sales conversation to have a quick complimentary remark on something that the prospect wears or that the prospect has in his office, such as a trophy or a painting or an outstanding piece of furniture. However, you should not dwell very long on this because if you do, you will be sidetracked and you will lose valuable time that should be spent for the sale.

43

After you have made a powerful opening statement that arouses attention and desire to learn what you have to offer, then ask questions which plant the proper answers. (This, you'll recognize, is the free energy way to sell.) Here let me give credit to the sales training which put me on the right road; given to me by the Fuller Brush Company. The principles they taught me years ago are still true today. If a salesman does not do anything additionally than to follow the sales pattern established by the Fuller Brush Company so many, many years ago, and if he persists in this pattern, he cannot help but be successful.

I have fond memories of the five years I spent with this wonderful company that gave me and so many other men who could not get a job elsewhere the opportunity to make an excellent living while being in business for themselves. I speak of the time shortly after the depression; and I would like to add here that such an opportunity is possible only in America.

19—How Frank Ridge Of Washington, D.C. Opens Up With His Ground Rules

I met Frank Ridge at a Million Dollar Round Table convention in Banff some years ago and have had the pleasure of exchanging ideas with him many times since. Frank is an outstanding salesman with original ideas. I asked him to use my question-and-answer system and he told me later that as a result of it his sales had increased substantially.

I am grateful to him for permitting me to use his ground rules which, I believe, can be used effectively in many situations. These ground rules make clear to the prospect that Frank is a businessman who deserves respect and that what he has to say is important. These powerful words from Frank separate the men from the boys right from the beginning of the interview:

"Mr. Jones, in all fairness to you and to myself I think we ought to establish some basic ground rules. That way you'll have a very clear idea of what you can expect from me and you'll know what I in turn can expect from you.

"In the first place, before I would expect you or anyone else for that matter to buy any life insurance from me, there are four basic requirements which should be met. The first one is, there must be a very clear need for this insurance. After discussing your situation with you and evaluating it I may in my own mind think that you need it. Now, ordinarily I have a very good opinion of my opinion but in this case it isn't worth two cents. You must be the one to determine whether or not you need it. You're the doctor.

"Let's assume for the moment that you need it, so we go on to the second requirement.

"In my book this is the most important one of them all, this is the one that makes Sammy run, this is the one that's made this country what it is today. It's a factor called *want*. In other words this need that you have has to be of a sufficiently compelling nature so that you won't be satisfied unless it's taken care of. We see a great deal of evidence around us of how important this factor called *want* is. Why, half of the cars on the road in America today were purchased because people wanted them and certainly not because they needed them. Heaven knows, the cars they traded in were quite adequate for transportation. You may wonder at this point just what kind of a nut I am. After all, this product called life insurance is not easy to sell to begin with and why do I make it so hard on myself? I do it for a very simple and a very good reason. If you buy any insurance from me, I'm going to expect you to keep it for the next twenty or thirty years. I want it to be a purchase which is based on good solid ground. We have provided two good bases for this structure and I think the next two that we outline to you will prove that this is going to be a very solid structure.

"All right, let's assume you need it and let's assume you want it. Obviously you expect me to come up with some kind of a solution. My solution to your problem has to be clearly the best possible solution. If you can, on your own, figure out something which is just as good—it doesn't have to be better, mind you—then what do you need me for?

"And so we move on to the last requirement, and probably the second most important one. As you well know, we aren't giving insurance away. There are dollars involved. We call it a premium. Here too, I feel very strongly about this concept of your calling the shots. You know if you and I were friends of twenty years standing, I wouldn't have the right to tell you that you can afford this or can't afford it. But under the circumstances, since we've just met, I certainly don't have that right. You and you alone are the judge as to whether or not you can afford it. Now is that fair enough?"

He has little choice; of course, he has to agree that our ground rules are fair, and we proceed.

PART III

Selling Is Knowing Human Nature

20--To Write, To Phone Or To See In Person

In selling, the difference between work and a game resulting in a sale is often the simple decision of either writing a letter, making a phone call or seeing the client or prospect in person. Let me give you an example.

During an interview, Mr. Prospect insists that he get a written proposal. He refuses to take the medical examination which would enable me to furnish him with a written proposal signed by the president of the insurance company. The prospect is firm in his demand. He wants a written proposal. I have no choice then but to go back to my office and complete such a proposal.

Now the proposal is finished. What next? Shall I mail it, shall I phone the prospect after I have mailed it to him to get his reaction, or shall I deliver it to him in person? Should I phone the prospect to make an appointment to deliver the proposal? If I do this he might just say, "Why don't you just put it in the mail so I have a chance to study it?" It is better to anticipate this reaction immediately and use the following approach:

"Mr. Prospect, I have your proposal. I was thinking of putting it in the mail to you; however, there are several points I know you will want to ask me about. And these points need some special explanation. I will be in your neighborhood tomorrow morning or the following day in the afternoon. It would only take me a few minutes to drop off the proposal and to explain these two points to you."

If I use this procedure, I give myself a chance to make the sale. If I just put it in the mail, then I have to wait for a reply from the prospect and this reply might never come. The fact that he had asked me for a proposal means most likely, however, that he is comparing my rates with those of another agent. If that is the case, I have no way to defend myself when the judge and the jury are one and the same person making the decision. So it is very essential that I anticipate what my prospect will say.

I should also try to close him. I should always do something that will enable me to get closer to the sale. I could call the prospect and say, "I am delighted, Mr. Prospect, that I have your proposal and it looks much better than I had anticipated. However, I would like to make sure that the figures I have furnished with the proposal will be absolutely correct, and that you will have a standby option on these figures guaranteed for at least three months." I will now shoot for the medical examination.

"Mr. Prospect, has anyone rejected you for life insurance lately? I would very much like our traveling examiner to stop by your office tomorrow morning or, if more convenient, at your home tomorrow night, to make sure that the rates I quoted you will be available to you. There is no obligation for you but it will obligate the insurance company."

What have I lost in trying this approach at this time? I cannot write the policy without his getting the medical examination, so why not get over this hurdle as soon as possible? Eventually I will get my way. I always feel that once I have an investment of my time with a certain prospect, I will give it all I have to make sure that his time is not wasted and that my time is not wasted.

I can recite the cases of many clients who would never have passed their medical examinations if they had been delayed at that time. Because of this technique of mine, many families are enjoying the benefits of life insurance today. Many children have been educated and many homes have been paid off because of my insistence that the medical examination be completed right away. While I was pushing for the medical examination, my competitor was furnishing meaningless figures. My thinking in these situations is best described in my book, *How I Sell $12,000,000 Worth of Life Insurance Year after Year*, in the Chapter, "Seven Little Words That Can Protect You From Failure." (See excerpt in the Appendix.)

The decision to phone, to write or to see in person should not be made lightly. If I put thought into what I do, my results will show it. This is particularly true when I make a proposal. Many times I have gotten business where other agents have left proposals with a prospect. These proposals were on ready-made forms. All my competitor had to do was fill in the numbers. I very seldom leave a proposal of this type. I feel that every one of my prospects is a special and very important person. When I work for him, he is the most important person on my mind. He deserves my best. Why should any type form proposal be what he should have?

When I prepare a proposal it will be specially made for him and it will be specially typed for him. It might not be a beautiful job in the eyes of my colleagues, but I want my prospect to know that it has been prepared with special care and with him in mind. This also applies when I have to write a letter.

If I write a sales letter, I am substituting myself. The letter should leave the door open for my future visit to explain my proposition or it should prepare the prospect for a medical examination. This is best illustrated in Chapter 63, "What To Do After An Interview."

Very often instead of a lengthy letter, I write a very short note simply stating:
"Dear John,

"Enclosed find a resume of our recent discussion. I know that you will have some questions and I will be visiting with you shortly to answer them for you."

I then enclose a conference memorandum with the letter. This conference memorandum is a complete but not elaborate synopsis of my sales procedure, re-stating what I tried to do to make the sale. This conference memorandum has been a great assistance to me in improving my closing ratio.

21—The Case Of The Floor Coverer

I will never forget the case of Robert Frank, owner of a thriving floor covering business in San Rafael, California. I do not remember who gave me the lead. I believe it came from a newspaper clipping relating a little news about the company and its founder and president, Mr. Robert Frank.

I tried to reach Mr. Frank on the phone several times, but I could never find him in. When I finally did find him in his office, he would not accept the call. But this time, since I had become very friendly with his secretary over the phone, she told me that a good time to see him was early in the morning about 8:00, that he was generally in his office at that time and not too busy. The following morning at 8:00 I was in Mr. Frank's office. Sure enough, he was agreeable to see me.

He said, "You are the tenth insurance man who has been trying to sell me, but I am telling you the same as I told every-body else. If you want to make me a proposal for $25,000 of whole life insurance, I will compare it with all these others I have here in my desk," and he pulled out a whole batch of beautifully drawn up proposals.

51

I said, "Mr. Frank, you have been very successful in the floor covering business. May I ask you just one question? When someone calls your office to get an appraisal on a floor covering job, do you quote a price over the phone or do you send out an estimator?"

He said, "Naturally we send out someone to look over the job."

Then I replied, "That is exactly what I wanted you to say, Mr. Frank, because as a fair businessman I presume that you are serious in getting the exact rate on a $25,000 policy, unless of course you are just kidding me."

"Naturally."

"In that case, Mr. Frank, I am quite sure that you would not object if I have our estimator come by your office tomorrow morning at 8:00 AM to measure you for your life expectancy."

Mr. Frank gave me the usual assurances that he just had his own physical from his own physician and that he was in perfect health.

I said, "Yes, Mr. Frank, I agree to that, but in the floor covering business you do not accept the appraisals of your competitors, do you? What we want is the appraisal of our own physician who is responsible to the insurance company. Your physician is responsible to you."

Mr. Frank agreed to have our examiner come by at 8:00 the following morning. Since I felt I had a very good prospect and since there was such tremendous competition involved, I went back the following morning and waited until the doctor was finished with the examination.

I caught the doctor on his way out about 8:30 AM and he told me, "Mr. Frank is in good shape."

I went into Mr. Frank's office and told him the good news. "Mr. Frank, now if you want to put a binder on this coverage we can do so at once, because it will still take a month or two to get the final approval from the insurance company."

I pulled out an application and completed the questions with him. Mr. Frank was a pilot and he was quite an accomplished one—and proud of it. I completed the aviation form and included an extra premium for flying in my rate card collections. It was not easy to get a check from Mr. Frank for the first monthly premium, but he finally agreed and I promised

52

I would be back to see him in about a month or so, at which time I would try to do a little estate planning for him.

During our discussions, I found out that his affairs were not in the best of order. He had a series of policies that had not been coordinated in any form whatsoever. In fact, he had me look at several where I noticed that his youngest daughter was not even named as beneficiary of a policy. I suggested that until his estate planning was completed in a coordinated form, he should name this youngest daughter the only contingent beneficiary on the new insurance.

Three days went by. I opened the newspaper one morning. There was the headline: "Plane Crashes Near Monterey, California—One Survivor." I read the article. My client, Mr. Robert Frank, was one of the victims. He, his wife and another man were killed in their private plane which had crashed in the ocean. The wife of the friend was able to save her life by swimming ashore.

The Frank case turned out to be a classical estate situation. There were two wills which did not properly work together. Mr. Frank had left his business to his wife, but Mrs. Frank had left everything after her death to her estate. But she was held to have survived Mr. Frank in the plane crash. The business, because of poor estate planning, was completely wrecked after three to four years. Two Frank sons who had been employed in the business were actually running the business for the bank trustee appointed under Mrs. Frank's will.

The widow who survived the crash sued for the loss of her husband. The little Frank girl who had been disinherited in all Mr. Frank's policies was the beneficiary of the policy that I had written.

This case proved to me what value a good job of estate planning could have had for the Frank family. But it also proved to me that a proposal left with a client is a worthless piece of paper, and that as life insurance men we have an obligation to do the job properly by producing the actual merchandise for our customer and giving him the chance to put it into effect for the benefit of his loved ones.

22—Motivation—Is Free Energy

Using examples such as the Frank case or others like it is the best type of motivation—and you need that in selling. Such stories are an important tool in demonstrating a point and in creating the atmosphere for decision making. In my opinion, motivating stories are most essential if you wish to obtain favorable results in your selling endeavors. In my early selling career, I had to use the stories of actual cases that my associates had experienced. In the course of time I was able to use my own cases. Naturally, in a history of selling spanning more than a quarter of a century, I have seen the impossible can and will happen.

The motivating stories that are most important are the ones you use in the closing. You can say to a man, "Well, this or that can happen to you. You could be killed in your automobile on your way home tonight," but it is much better to make this point by relating an actual story. Many times a news clipping about prominent people can demonstrate a point well. One of the latest closing stories is that of Mr. Charles Austerland.

Charles Austerland came to my office but he was a very difficult man to pin down in reaching a decision. I was lucky, however, he would listen to me. He gave me a check for $40, which was the monthly premium on a $50,000 term policy to protect his wife and six children. A week or so later, I received a memo from the insurance company stating that Mr. Austerland's check had bounced. This was the first check, and the remaining monthly payments would be paid for out of the check deduction plan automatically from his bank account to the insurance company.

I immediately tried to phone Mr. Austerland and to ask him to give me another check, but my various attempts to reach him either at work or at home were unsuccessful. So I wrote a letter to the Austerlands explaining the circumstances. When I thought of the six children, I said to my bookkeeper,

"Margot, won't you please write out a check for $40 and send it to the insurance company. I am sure that Mr. Austerland is on a vacation or somewhere; otherwise, we would have heard from him."

Four weeks went by. There was a telephone call. Mrs. Austerland was on the phone and she said: "Mr. Bach, I just want you to know that it is all right to put my husband's check through at this time. It is good now."

Mrs. Austerland sounded rather uneasy over the phone. I didn't know what the reason was but I was soon to find out.

The following day, two gentlemen came to my office. They introduced themselves. They were the two brothers of Mr. Austerland. They asked if they could speak to me privately in my office. I invited them in and they informed me that their brother, Charles, had been killed in an automobile accident the first day of his vacation and all the children and Mrs. Austerland were in the hospital.

Now I understood why Mrs. Austerland sounded so anxious the day before and I also understood why I could not reach them by mail or by phone. They wanted to make a claim on the policy now, and they were quite concerned whether or not it was in force. I assured them that the policy was in full force. Mrs. Austerland and her six children are now living on the $100,000 that this $50,000 policy provided through the double idemnity provision.

By changing only the name, I use this sales story to emphasize not only the importance of putting insurance in effect but also the importance of doing business with me because I do the little extra things that often make the difference between protection being in force and not in force.

Another motivating story that I use—and I use many of them to demonstrate points I want to emphasize—is the case of Ed Devine, a lawyer. Ed had been examined for life insurance and after several additional tests finally qualified for an $80,000 policy. Since his office was in the same building as mine, I felt it was very easy for me to place this policy.

I was to see Ed early one morning but he told me that he was too busy to give me any time. He was engaged in a trial which would probably take four weeks and during this period of time he couldn't take time out for anything. He asked me to just postpone everything until after the completion of the trial.

What could I do? Here is a man who works in the same building. I see him in the elevator all the time. But I have to do what he tells me.

Four weeks went by. This was also the expiration of the medical examination. I immediately went into Ed's office. I asked if he would have a few minutes to take care of the insurance now. Ed told me that he had not yet finished his trial.

55

There was some delay and he asked if I would see him in a week.

I said, "Ed, your medical examination is expiring today. If you wouldn't mind, I would like to have you sign the health certificate that your health has not changed and, if possible, give me a binder so the insurance company is on the risk immediately, until you are ready to make your final decision regarding your policy."

Ed said "I won't sign a thing. You just wait until a week from now and then we'll decide on the whole thing."

I walked back to my office. This was on Friday afternoon. The following Monday morning when I came to the office, the elevator man said:

"Karl, do you know what happened to Ed Devine?"

I said, "What happened?"

"Ed Devine dropped dead on Sunday at the Forty-Niner game."

It is very essential that you use motivating stories of this type. If you do not have any of your own, use paper clippings that demonstrate the tragedy of life. But never let your own client be the one who dies. Always show what has happened to others. Many decisions are made through the heart and not necessarily through the pocketbook.

The motivating story, used at exactly the right time, is a very, very powerful weapon in our arsenal. However, a salesman has to keep in mind that he has come back to the track that led him to tell the motivating story. In working with other salesmen, I have often found that they tell their story but then forget why they were telling it.

Yes, it is essential that we keep our mind firmly focused on our objective at all times. Our objective, need I remind you, is to make the sale.

Another trap we should avoid when telling such motivating stories is the trap of repeating the same story over and over until we become stale in relating it. Every time we tell a story, we must tell it as if it is new, and we have to be excited about it. We have to be like the actor who every night on the stage gives a new and brilliant performance. The fact that we have heard the story from our own lips so often before should never interfere with the telling of it again. And, don't forget, conviction and enthusiasm are needed to get results.

23—Never Refuse A Prospect Or A Client The Benefit Of Your Time—Regardless Of What Is In It For You!

Harry Smith, an old client, carried with me all his insurance for his little store which he operated together with his wife; but I could never sell him much life insurance regardless of how hard I tried. Just a short time before he called me and asked me to visit him I had tried to sell him again, but was unsuccessful. When he called me for a visit, he said that he needed to see me very much, but I did not need to bring anything along. He just wanted to talk to me, he said. I immediately agreed to visit with him, regardless of the fact that he really was not a prospect for me and that the time, most likely, would be wasted.

I also did not ask him to come to my office, which is what I generally do, because I felt that he wanted me really to visit him at his business. When I arrived at his store, I was fortunate that he and his wife were the only ones behind the counter. I had never met his wife and I could discern a deep devotion between the two of them from the glances they exchanged.

Yes, he did have a problem. His problem was that over the years he had stocked his business with merchandise. Every nickel that he was making went back on the shelves and, because of inflation, the replacement cost of all his merchandise was three times its cost ten years ago when he started his business. What had bothered him was the fire insurance coverage on his merchandise, the amount of which was based on his cost. If he should have a fire he would not collect the value of his inventory but only what he had actually paid for it. I told him, much to his relief, that we would take care of this problem. There was no need to lose $90,000. And now I had my opening—and I knew it—at this moment to sell the life insurance that he so badly needed.

I asked him, "Do you think that, God forbid, if something should happen to you, your wife would be able to run this business alone?"

He said, "Never. We are working too hard now, the two of us. She would have to sell it."

I said, "Now, this is the case. The loss that your wife would receive on the merchandise is going to be even greater, because she will probably have to liquidate the business, and then she will get, not 50%, not 30%, but probably 10¢ on the dollar, unless we take care of it with life insurance."

This statement was sufficient finally to open the eyes of my prospect to visualize a much larger policy than I had previously tried to place on him. He had written his own prescription. And I am reminded of this simple fact: first find the loss and then find how you can insure it. Then you have a good prospect.

24—During The Sales Interview—Remember!

1. Truth is your greatest source of power.

2. Anticipate his problems.

3. Determine solutions in advance (take his file home and study it before each interview).

4. Consider your prospect's point of view by putting yourself in his place.

5. Be completely frank and think clearly.

6. Don't show you dominate, even when you do.

7. Enthusiasm will energize and light humor will ease tension.

8. Let your prospect do the talking which you direct by having asked the questions for which you need his answers (study all our set of Free Energy questions).

9. Have patience while you listen. Keep your mouth shut.

RESULT:
A sale becomes a purchase in your prospect's mind. He will tell his friends he gave you his life insurance business. Do you mind?

25—The Art Of Listening Refined

Many sales are lost by salesmen who listen to their prospects, so to say, with only one ear. They listen while the prospect talks and they are meanwhile manufacturing a reply without giving full attention to what the prospect is telling them and what the prospect really means. Through this type of listening, they very often miss the most important points that the prospect tries to convey, and while missing these most important points, they most often miss the sale along with it.

I know that I have personally been guilty of this type of listening throughout my sales career and quite often I catch myself thinking of a reply that I am going to use when the prospect has not yet completely finished his thoughts.

I remember one case in particular where a prospect told me that had I let him finish talking, I would have heard that he was going to buy. He was first going to explain to me, so he said, why he was not going to buy and then he was going to tell me why he still had to buy my produce, as there was no way out for him. I am quite sure you have all found yourselves in similar situations. We must learn to be patient while listening and pay full attention to what the prospect intends to say. We should keep our eyes on the prospect's lips, be veritably interested and constitute a good audience for him. By being a good audience, we will without a doubt help the prospect to like us, and that, naturally, will also help in establishing a client relationship.

26—It Pays To Be A Good Listener

The Case Of The Camera Store Owner Listening Is The Key:

One of my associates, Al Hill, who for many years has been a multi-million dollar producer of life insurance, has been specializing in business life insurance for a long time. In my opinion, he is one of the most dedicated life insurance professionals in the business. However, he has much untapped sales power which could easily double or triple his production.

Al had made several calls in an effort to sell the owner of several large camera stores, Mr. Edward Gaines. Mr. Gaines had qualified as an A-1 risk, but Al could not get a decision from him in time to place the insurance. He decided to bring me in the case before the door was shut completely. Al asked me if I could make the call one day on our way home from work. I readily agreed.

When I work jointly with another agent, I usually ask what has been said to the prospect about me, as well as why it is good for the prospect to meet with me. (Cf., Chapter 48.) In most cases, I insist that my colleague sell the prospect on the idea of coming to my office. If this can be accomplished, then the sale is often made much easier.

In this particular case, I made an exception and we stopped at the prospect's place of business. It was nearly closing time. Mr. Gaines was very friendly toward me and asked my associate if he would mind if he met with me alone the following morning. This request by the prospect seemed very unusual. It had never happened to me before, but Al agreed. He knew this was his last chance to make the sale.

The following morning I arrived at the appointed time. Mr. Gaines let me into his office and after a few casual remarks asked me if I would mind listening to a tape recording he had made of my associate's sales presentation. I was surprised. Something like this had never happened to me. Gaines started the tape and left me alone listening to Al's sales presentation.

It turned out to be an outstanding lecture on the value of business life insurance. This lecture would have been well received at a meeting of CPA's, trust officers, CLU's or attorneys. It was an excellent job. It covered every point on the subject of business life insurance.

Al had planned a very intelligent program for Mr. Gaines. The prospect had a son 16 years old who was working part time in the business. By increasing the son's salary sufficiently each year, enough money would be released to pay for the life insurance policy, thus creating, in effect, tax deductible dollars for that purpose. But the one thing that Al did not discover was the fact that Mr. Gaines' son was Mrs. Gaines' stepson—a very important point in the scheme of things.

After I had listened to the tape for about ten minutes, Mr. Gaines returned. He asked what I thought of Al's presentation. My reply was that it was an oustanding job, but in my opinion the plan outlined by Al was unsuitable for Mr. Gaines. He readily agreed. The following dialogue developed:

"Mr. Gaines, please shut off this machine," I said, "and let me ask you a few questions. What do you think life insurance can accomplish for you and your family? What did you have in mind when you took your life insurance physical examination?"

60

"If I should die, my wife couldn't run this business," he said, "and I want her to be taken care of."

"How much life insurance did you intend to buy at this time?"

"How much is $100,000 worth?"

"That's only $250 per month."

We closed the case for this amount and everyone was happy with the outcome. My associate could have done this business alone had he used the right questions and done more listening and a bit less talking. This case was as simple as a case can be. Yes, simplicity speeds selling.

27—The Proper Use Of Your Voice

Two people can say the same words, the same sentences, and get different results. The reason is that the manner in which they present an idea and what they put into their voices create different reactions.

A salesman who gives a sales talk in a monotonous tone, whose delivery is dreary, will have an audience which is only waiting for him to shut up and get out. But a salesman who can create desire, anxiety, humor and expectation with his emotions properly inserted into his sales talk, will have the prospect asking for more—and an audience which will be working with him rather than against him.

Getting the prospect into a happy frame of mind early in the interview is using free energy in a most intelligent fashion. It creates a chain reaction of free energy.

I often ask the question: "What do you hate about life insurance, Mr. Prospect?" and I kind of laugh. It appears that if I have a smile in my voice, it somehow takes the seriousness out of the question and helps me to get a good reaction from the prospect—his mind seems to open up. By letting him do the talking, I can record valuable information which will help me further throughout the interview.

When I want to emphasize a point of value to the prospect, I become very excited so he cannot help but feel this excitement and become energized. Frequently, I will speak very softly and very slowly. Many times I pause in order to let what I have just said sink in and I let silence prevail. There seems to be a lot of power in silence.

Most of these things I do instinctively because of the many sales interviews I have had over the years. I recommend that every salesman try his own variations and he will de:.elop a style to fit his personality and will create his desired results. However, it takes practice and the more sales talks you will give, the more opportunity you will have to perfect the proper use of your voice.

28—Everybody Knows Somebody Who Needs Life Insurance

The Lead From The Massuer To The Man Who Wanted To Lose Weight:

Every Wednesday afternoon (naturally with some exceptions) I play ping pong at a local health club located across the street from my office. If time allows, I ask for a massage. While having fun and recreation, I cannot help but make the acquaintance of some prominent local businessmen who also take time off for the same reasons I do.

One day the masseur said to me, "Karl, I massaged a man today who said that he is losing weight so that he can qualify at low rates for life insurance. I will give you his name, but please don't tell him that I referred you."

A referred lead is generally not very good if you cannot refer to the donor. Nonetheless, I took down the details from the masseur by completing one of my prospect cards. I always carry blank cards in my pocket. I went to work at once. I never let a lead get stale.

My objective prior to the call was to make an appointment with the prospect. Our conversation progressed somewhat as follows:

"Good morning, Mr. Goodfellow, this is Karl Bach. I am a buyer of life insurance. My business is buying life insurance for people and I have a lot of experience with people . . ."

The prospect interrupted me. "I am sorry. I won't be able to see you. And I am not interested in life insurance."

I proceeded: "Mr. Goodfellow, you won't have to see me to get the benefit of my experience as a buyer of life insurance unless you want to. Have you ever been turned away by a life insurance company?"

He said, "No."

"Since this is the case, would you object if Dr. Holzman, our traveling examiner, would stop by your office tomorrow morning or sometime this evening at your home to measure your life expectancy. I will have a report back to you on the results in about three to four weeks and I can assure you it will be worth your while."

This approach hit him by surprise. He agreed to have the doctor stop by his office, provided I would put him under no obligation. I always have a blank life insurance application on my desk. The prospect answered all the questions for me readily. At the end of three weeks, San Francisco Life approved this application for $100,000 and so notified me. I prefer this notice of approval to the actual policy unless the sale is fully completed.

Whenever I receive such a notice of approval, I become very excited because I now have the merchandise available that only good health and not money alone can buy. I immediately called Mr. Goodfellow. He did not want to see me. "Call me in two weeks."

When the two weeks had passed, I was on the phone with him again. The following conversation took place:

"Mr. Goodfellow, as I told you two weeks ago, you qualified as an A-1 risk for our company for $100,000."

Mr. Goodfellow said, "I am sorry. I cannot see you. I am leaving for Europe in a week and I will be gone for about six months."

My answer was, "Mr. Goodfellow, you won't have to see me until you return, or, for that matter, you won't ever have to see me at any time. Do you have a pencil handy? Would you please write down the number "20,406"? This is your policy number. With this number and your check for $1,206 we can bind the insurance company to cover you for $100,000 for the next six months. Or, If you wish, you can let us have your check for $2,400 and we will provide coverage for the next twelve months. If you would not object, I will send my secretary down right away to pick up your check. You will also have to put your name on the application form."

He replied, "Why didn't you tell me the last time you called that we could do it this way?"

My secretary picked up his application and the check for the first six months premium. To this date, my client and I have

San Francisco Life *Insurance Company*

FOUNDED BY KARL BACH

DATE NOVEMBER 6, 19

TO MARSH-KENT CORP.

NOTICE OF APPROVAL. WE ARE PREPARED TO ISSUE THIS POLICY ON THE FOLLOWING BASIS:

POLICY NO.	POLICY DATE	AGE	SEX	AMOUNT	PLAN/BENEFIT	ANNUAL PREMIUM	YR. CHG.	FORM NO.	APL	MODE
20,406	PA	42	M	$100,000	Pro.95	$2,384.00	23	70	Y	A
I. MARTIN GOODFELLOW					PF	10.00				
				50,000	OPAI	---	73	R1008		

D.B.

BILLING TO

OWNER	THE INSURED	RATING	STD		Tot. Am.	2,394.00
				Semi Ann.	1,220.94
				Quarterly	622.44
				Monthly	209.48
				Ser. Mat.	203.49

| | B.A. | AGT. NO. | SHARE | CONT'R |
| AGENTS | Marsh-Kent | 387 | 100% | 4 |

NOTE:

IS THE LAST DAY FOR DELIVERY, AFTER WHICH ADDITIONAL EVIDENCE OF INSURABILITY WILL BE REQUIRED

| REASONS FOR RATINGS ▲ | HEALTH | OCC | CONFIDENTIAL | BENEFITS NOT GRANTED ▼ | B.I. | W.P. | G.I.R. | OTHER |

$ 2,394.00 PREMIUM DUE

$_____ RECEIVED BY COMPANY

$ 2,394.00 BALANCE DUE

$

OVERAGE, WILL BE APPLIED TO FUTURE PREMIUMS UNLESS WE HAVE BEEN INSTRUCTED OTHERWISE.

[X] HAVE THE ____APPLICATION____ WHICH IS BOUND INTO THE POLICY AND THE LOOSE COPY DATED AND SIGNED **BEFORE** RELEASING POLICY. *IF ANY QUESTIONABLE OR UNFAVORABLE INFORMATION IS DEVELOPED HOLD THE POLICY AND NOTIFY THE HOME OFFICE IMMEDIATELY.*

[ ] RETURN EITHER THE ALTERNATE OR REGULAR POLICY FOR CANCELLATION. **DO NOT** DELIVER BOTH WITHOUT HOME OFFICE PERMISSION.

[ ] OTHER REQUIREMENTS:

AGENT: PLEASE ADVISE OF DELIVERY OR (IF NOT ALREADY DONE) TO ISSUE THE POLICY BY RETURNING ONE (1) COPY AND COMPLETING:

[ ] POLICY DELIVERED $_____ENCLOSED. CHECK DRAWN BY:

[ ] REISSUE AS FOLLOWS (OR NEW APPLICATION MAY BE ENCLOSED):

[ ] ISSUE AS SPECIFIED ABOVE.

[ ] CHANGE BILLING MODE OR ADDRESS AS NOTED ABOVE.

WRITING AGENT_____

FORM U104 (REV. 1067)

AGENT'S COPY

64

never met. But we have become very friendly over the telephone.

This proves that people will often buy if given the opportunity. Life insurance is a product already accepted by intelligent people. If you make it easy to buy and take away the mystery of it, you can add many easy sales to your weekly production. Yes, just the knowledge that people will buy will make many sales for you. We do not always have to work as hard as we seem to believe. The many thousands of salesmen who have worked for the last one hundred years have spread the seeds of desire for life insurance. Millions of people are waiting to be cultivated with the proper approach and the right salesman.

29—When The Prospect Says, "I Want To See My Attorney; I Want To Talk It Over With My CPA"

If the objection comes up, "I want to talk it over with my attorney," I simply say: "Mr. Prospect, do you know what law school your attorney graduated from?" Usually the prospect is surprised by this question and doesn't know the answer.

"Let's assume, Mr. Prospect, that he graduated from Harvard, one of the finest law schools. Do you know the one thing they do not teach even at Harvard, Mr. Prospect?"

The prospect wants to know.

"The one thing they do not teach at the Harvard Law School is business judgment. Do you agree?"

I use the same tactic when it comes to accountants.

"To buy or not to buy the life insurance that I have recommended, Mr. Prospect, is a business decision you must make. It is not a legal and it is not an accounting decision. Your attorney can only say one of two things in answer to your problem. He can say either you should buy the life insurance I recommend, or he can say you should not buy it. If you want him to say No—and I do not believe this is the case—why not tell me so yourself? I am convinced your attorney would never put negative advice in writing. Because if he did and something should happen to you, Mr. Prospect, your attorney could be held responsible by your family or by your corporation."

Here Is How Jack Kleiner Answers When The Client Says, "I Want To Talk It Over With My Accountant":

When the client says to me, "Jack I think the program that you presented is great, but I never do anything without my accountant," I answer: "Really, you don't do anything without your accountant?" (Let's assume he is a manufacturer of textiles.) "Every time you order piece goods you make a style or you put in cuttings, do you call your accountant first?" "No!" "Why not? Obviously, its because you're the businessman and you run your business.

"Now I'm asking you only to come to a sound business judgment. Do you like what I presented? Do you understand it? Do you like what it does for you? Wonderful.

"Now, I'm anxious to meet your accountant, but remember—we have to set the ground rules. He has your welfare at heart, and so do I. He's a professional and so am I. Now we'll take him only for one thing, the thing he does for you. When he audits your books, he tells you if your books are in balance, how much money you've made and so on. I want him to look at my program and say, 'Is it mathematically right?'

"I'm not really interested in whether he likes what it does for you. But if he's a man of sound business judgment—and this is quite important, I don't mean just an auditor—then he can tell you (what I'm sure you'll understand) how much the investments I'm asking you to make will do for you, in his opinion.

"Now if I'm mathematically correct, I want him to say so. If I'm mathematically incorrect, I want him to say so, too. And if he has a better way—remember, we're both interested in doing the right thing for you—if he has a better way for what I'm asking you to do, then I want him to say so because I'm always willing to learn. I doubt whether he'll know a better way, but if he does, wonderful. I'm always willing to learn.

"Now, remember, everything I've told you, you can only get if you can medically qualify, and you haven't done that for me yet because you just don't get insurance because you want it. So I'll have our doctor check you over. After you have qualified, I'll take care of all the details. Fair enough? And meanwhile, so that we can obligate the insurance company, write out a check for so much and so much."

Jack also uses the same argument when he gets the objection: "I want to talk it over with my lawyer."

30—The Case Of The Architect, The Lawyer And The CPA

There are exceptions to every rule. One of my rules is, when a client wants me to see his attorney, to make sure that the insurance is in force before I see the attorney. This has the advantage that it is not up to the attorney to decide what the client should buy. He will only be involved in the legal aspects.

But here is a case that is an exception. I had to see an attorney before I could put the insurance into effect. I made up my mind that the attorney would become an ally instead of an opponent.

Several attempts on a referred lead to a famous San Francisco architect failed to get me an appointment. I decided to make one last attempt, because I felt I had a real good prospect. Finally, the prospect suggested that I meet with him and his attorney at a given time. Naturally, I agreed. When I entered the lawyer's office, I felt I was entering the cold atmosphere of a mosque. My prospect had already arrived and so had the prospect's CPA.

The lawyer opened up: "What do you want to sell my client and how much?"

I answered: "Mr. Attorney, let me ask you a question. If your client stopped before a red light and a big overland bus plowed into him with fatal results, for how much would you sue the bus company?"

There was a deep silence in the room. Then the CPA spoke up. He started figuring the client's income and came up with a million and a half. The lawyer added: "Yes, a million and a half, at least."

After this, I simply said: "Gentlemen, I rest my case with you," and kept my mouth shut. We then settled for the amount of insurance the client could afford to buy.

The lawyer and the CPA have since referred some very valuable clients to me.

31—Exceptions Can Pay Off

This is another example where my intuition told me to make an exception and it paid off.

Bill Montague, my associate and one of the most outstanding life insurance professionals in the business, needed my assistance. We always help one another if the need arises. One of his prospects did not want to make a decision without his attorney.

Bill asked me if I knew Jack Ross, a local attorney. I did not. Bill felt that I would do better than he with the attorney and had me agree that we would make the call on this lawyer together. Here is the way I handled the situation.

When we came to the attorney's office, I noticed that he was a very busy man. There were papers and files all over the room. He was a man about 40 and weighed about 200 lbs. He had a very pleasing personality. I took the seat nearest the attorney and Bill sat across the room. My plan of action was to present the case to the attorney as if he himself were the prospect and not simply the lawyer of our prospect. Since this attorney was kind enough to give us his time, I opened the conversation like this.

"Mr. Attorney, we are taking your valuable time today to explain to you the kind of life insurance Bill Montague has recommended to your builder client. We don't know if you can bill the time we are talking to him or not. If you cannot, we would feel a lot better if you would start clocking us now and send us a bill for your charges."

Ross replied, "I appreciate your thoughts but I am working for the builder. Let's see what you have."

I then proceeded, "Mr. Ross, have you ever seen an x-ray of a life insurance policy? Do you know how life insurance works? Let me show you what it can do for you. What is the date of your birth?"

He gave me his date of birth and I went through our ledger sales talk (completely reprinted herein or available upon request). Jack Ross bought $80,000 of life insurance from us. We recommended that his builder client do likewise but we could never land the builder as our client, although he is still a prospect.

But, I had hit the jackpot! Since then, Jack Ross has become one of my greatest boosters and business-getters in town. In one year alone, as a result of his recommendations, I placed over three million dollars of life insurance. He is one of the city's best known tax attorneys and is doing work for many general practitioner lawyers and CPA's. The reason he recommends me,

PERMANENT LIFETIME PROTECTION⁻

Designed Exclusively For: _____

Designed by: __KARL BACH_____

Amount of Insurance $ __100,000_____   Annual Premium Deposit $ __2,341.00___

Year	Annual Premium Deposit	YEARLY DEPOSIT IS DIVIDED INTO TWO PARTS		Total Cash Value	Fully Paid-Up Insurance	Death Benefit
		Annual Net Cost	Increase in Cash Value			
1	2,341	2,341				100,000
2	2,341	1,541	800	800	2,500	100,000
3	2,341	141	2,200	3,000	9,000	100,000
4	2,341	141	2,200	5,200	15,100	100,000
5	2,341	41	2,300	7,500	21,100	100,000
TOTAL	11,705	4,205	7,500			
6	2,341	41	2,300	9,800	26,900	100,000
7	2,341	59CR	2,400	12,200	32,500	100,000
8	2,341	159CR	2,500	14,700	38,100	100,000
9	2,341	259CR	2,600	17,300	43,600	100,000
10	2,341	259CR	2,600	19,900	48,800	100,000
TOTAL	23,410	3,510	19,900			
11	2,341	359CR	2,700	22,600	53,900	100,000
12	2,341	359CR	2,700	25,300	58,700	100,000
13	2,341	459CR	2,800	28,100	63,500	100,000
14	2,341	559CR	2,900	31,000	68,300	100,000
15	2,341	659CR	3,000	34,000	73,000	100,000
TOTAL	35,115	1,115	34,000			
16	2,341	759CR	3,100	37,100	77,600	100,000
17	2,341	859CR	3,200	40,300	82,300	100,000
18	2,341	859CR	3,200	43,500	86,600	100,000
19	2,341	959CR	3,300	46,800	91,000	100,000
20	2,341	2,059CR	4,400	51,200	97,200	100,000
TOTAL	46,820	4,380CR	51,200			

AT AGE 65

M 35
LB30

Additional Benefits Available _____

Waiver of Premium: $ __69.00____ Annually

Accidental Death: $ __115.00__ Annually

Optional Method of Premium Deposits:

Monthly $ __204.84___   Quarterly $ __608.66__

Save-Matic $ __198.99__   Semi-Annual $ __1,193.91__

When your policy is issued, the amount of premium, all benefits and all values are fully guaranteed, as stated in the policy. They do not depend upon future earnings of the Company.

San Francisco Life Insurance Company

so he says, is that I stick to the business of life insurance and its basic function, and do not become involved in the practice of tax laws and other technicalities for which the attorney and the CPA are responsible.

32—Why Look For A New Mine When You Still Have Ore In Your Old Mine

Many salesmen, upon making a sale to a particular client, then look for another new client, without realizing that there is still tremendous potential for more business with their present client. Quite frequently all that is required to find more ore in the old mine is to dig a little deeper. And in our business, digging a little deeper means quite simply getting more information. Getting more information means asking more questions, to which, by the way, the client will gladly volunteer the answers.

In talking with one of my clients' wives the other day over the phone, I was told how unhappy she was to have to write so many checks for her husband's insurance premiums. She was thinking of canceling half the insurance. I gave her a very sympathetic ear because I don't know of anyone who likes to write checks for insurance premiums.

During this conversation, I asked her several questions and I learned that her father, a wealthy Eastern banker, had died several years ago and that she had just received a distribution of a large trust fund providing her with a sizable amount of income on which she had had to pay the income tax. It immediately occurred to me that here was a unique opportunity to recommend the use of short term trusts for their five children—trusts which could receive the income from this inheritance and this income could then be used to pay for the life insurance premiums about which she was complaining.

She liked the idea very much. Their attorney agreed with my recommendations. The saving in taxes is now being used to provide for a sizable life insurance policy on her to cover her estate tax liability on the inherited property left to her by her father.

Digging in the old mine deeper can work in various ways. Frequently, there are other family members who need life insurance. Many times when we are selling personal life insurance, we

70

discover a business situation that cries for the uses of life insurance; and just as many times when we are selling business life insurance; and just as many times when we are selling business insurance, we discover the need for personal life insurance that might have been overlooked completely.

The variety of possibilities is tremendous. The important thing is not to walk away from your mine until you have all the ore that you can economically acquire. It is so much easier to continue mining where you are already established than to jump sporadically over the geography to locate a new mine.

33—Why Do I Need It: The Case Of The 63-Year-Old Widower

When I called on Mr. Jackson, a 63-year-old widower, he informed me that his estate was just then being planned by an estate planning specialist. He was interested in getting my ideas, but there wasn't a chance to do business with me. The specialist was a very close friend of the prospect's son, a young attorney, who was indebted to the specialist for having referred legal business to him. The prospect had lost his wife recently and had told one of my clients that he had to come up with $890,000 to pay death taxes in the next few months. What a good life insurance salesman could have done at one time! I decided on the simplest approach of all.

"Mr. Jackson, only a small percentage of men age 63 I call on can qualify for life insurance. Here is what I would like to do for you today. I would like to line up for you the life insurance that you might possibly want to consider. In order to do so, I would like to get an option for you for one of my companies and I would like to get this option for you without any obligation on your part. Your estate might have to be planned with or without life insurance. Is there any reason why you might not be able to qualify?"

The prospect assured me of his outstanding health.

I continued, "In this case, Mr. Jackson, you won't object to my making a mortality study and measuring your life expectancy."

I knew that I had to be strong here and sell the only thing that made sense—the medical examination. Although I knew that later on an x-ray and electrocardiogram, as well as a second examination would be needed, at this particular interview I arranged for only the one examination. I called my regular examiner from the prospect's office and set up the date. I departed with the agreement that Mr. Jackson would see me in three or four weeks and give me the opportunity to present my plan to him then.

The medical examination is the gateway to the sale. The verbal battle to get this medical examination was not exactly as easy as explained here, but my determination to sell this examination was the free energy to pave the way for the final success in this case.

The doctor and Mr. Jackson met and the examination looked very favorable. I immediately called Mr. Jackson and said:

"Mr. Jackson, I am delighted to tell you that the doctor said that you looked pretty good for a man 63. In fact, unusually good. This makes me very happy, but unfortunately we need some additional tests. But, please, do not worry. It will be necessary for you to see our Dr. Morgan on Wednesday at 10:00 AM for an x-ray and an electrocardiogram and some additional information. I am sure that it will come out all right.

"Why is this necessary?" said Mr. Jackson.

I replied, "If you were the insurance company, Mr. Jackson, what would you do if you were to gamble on a man aged 63?"

"I can see your point," said Mr. Jackson and agreed to the date for the final tests.

I applied for $500,000 worth of life insurance and was fortunate to get a standard issue in spite of a borderline blood pressure coupled with a history of elevated blood pressure. However, $500,000 was all I could get at a standard rate.

When I went into Mr. Jackson's office for our next appointment, his son the lawyer was present, as well as his daughter. The lawyer started the conversation:

"Our estate planner came to the conclusion that my father does not need any life insurance. What do you have to say, Mr. Bach?"

I answered: "I have to agree that your father does not need any life insurance, and I would like to add that nobody needs life insurance. In fact, life insurance is always bought to benefit someone other than the insured. But let me ask you, why does your father carry the life insurance that he now has in the amount of $380,000?"

The lawyer explained to me that this covered part of his father's taxes. The remaining $600,000 could easily be raised with various corporations his father owned.

I asked if he would have been a good businessman to have had more insurance on his mother's life. He agreed to this. Turning to his father, I continued:

"Mr. Jackson you must have been a good businessman all your life to amass such a large estate, and I am sure you have taken advantage of any good deal if there was one."

"You bet," said Mr. Jackson.

"Now, Mr. Jackson, please take a pencil and multiply $31,000 by 15," I said.

"That's $465,000," answered Mr. Jackson.

"You are correct," I replied. This is all you can pay us for your $500,000 policy."

I pulled the policy out of my inside pocket and handed it to the lawyer.

"That is all you can pay us for the $500,000, Mr. Jackson, if you live 15 years. Isn't it good business on your part to know that an insurance company will gamble on your life for more than 15 years? Wouldn't you want the insurance company to make a lot of money on you so that this policy becomes a lousy deal for you? But when it becomes a lousy deal for you, you know that you will live. By the way, because of your blood pressure history, this $500,000 is all I could get for you at this rate."

There was dead silence in the room. Mr. Jackson broke the silence and asked his son, the lawyer, how the policy should be owned and who the beneficiary should be. They couldn't come to a decision on this point, so I suggested that for $2790 we could bind the insurance company to the risk and decide on the final disposition of these small points within the next 60 days.

The father gave me his personal check. The details were settled to the satisfaction of all in another interview. At that time, I added the lawyer and his sister to my list of clients. At no time was there a mention of the competing estate planner.

In many such cases where insurance is needed to provide cash for estate settlement cost, I have quoted, with the permission of the client (and will continue to quote) an actual case with great success. No doubt it helped when I used it with the widower and his attorney son. Here it is:

I am very grateful to a dear friend, Mr. Carl W. Stern, President of Lawson, Williams & Stern, Inc., a corporate member of the New York Stock Exchange, for the following ideas.

When I called upon Mr. Stern again in 1965, he immediately asked me to raise his family's life insurance coverage. I was rather surprised because most members of the investment community at that time were very anti-insurance and very bullish on common stocks. On the other hand, Mr. Stern had foreseen the *future* development of the international and internal financial crises as early as 1963, and by 1965 was accelerating his preparations for protection.

He said, "I am putting my portfolios in a more liquid position at this time and since that means we are going to have increased cash and equivalent, perhaps for several years, I see no reason why some of this cash should not be used advantageously in life insurance, obtaining substantial additional protection for my family during the time we carry it."

He added, "I see life insurance as a *series of options* one of which you are *forced* to choose each time a premium is payable. (Of course, I realize the program can also be changed during the premium year.) Just as a bond portfolio may have certain maturities each year which *require* reinvestment decision, so should the owner decide about his insurance at least once a year. When conditions change and cash is needed or must be conserved, the 'insurance bond' does not have to be liquidated. The performance of the 'insurance bond' will continue while the insurance company itself provides the loan value at a guaranteed rate of 5%, either to pay current and future premiums or to be available for other purposes of the owner. If conditions require a change in the insurance program, the insurance contract allows the insured to take paid up insurance on a guaranteed schedule contained in the policy. Meanwhile, the insured's family has greatly increased protection in the event of his (premature) death."

Last but not least, Mr. Stern pointed out to me that, when the need for cash arises, having the insurance protection and its loan provisions permit him to tie up or to raise less cash for tax or reserve purposes.

34—Needs vs. Wants

When I entered the life insurance business, I was taught by my contemporaries to sell "needs." If a man dies, his family needs income; the children need to be educated; and so on. I sold these needs for a long time; and then suddenly I realized that this could be wrong, and I thought that a better way to sell would be to create a desire, and then sell the "wants." It didn't take me long to realize that selling "wants" was a lot easier than selling "needs."

At that time, television sets were first introduced to the American public; and although until that time nobody had television because it wasn't produced, it gradually became so that everybody wanted a television set—not because they needed one but because of the simple desire. And when later on color television was produced, the people who had the black and white sets suddenly became dissatisfied. They did not suddenly need color television sets but they wanted them. And so it is with the "need" selling versus the "want" selling.

I learned that the American family and the American businessman will buy what they want; but before they can want something, they have to have a desire for it. And that is where we as salesmen come in. If we are able to create the desire in our prospect for our product, then there should be no problem in furnishing the product to the prospect.

My entire sales system has been geared to creating this desire and that is what free energy selling is all about.

PART IV

Selling Success Can Be For All

35—Ten Fundamental Objectives For Each Day

1. To arrange, on a firm basis, breakfast and luncheon appointments with prospects.

2. To set up at least one appointment for a medical examination for a prospect with whom I have discussed life insurance. This is the gateway to a sale.

3. To arrange for the delivery of a policy by appointment. My client is entitled to this courtesy and my time is too valuable to "drop in" if my client is not ready and expecting to see me.

4. To obtain from every client the names of at least three potential prospects, in order to continue to build new links in my ever-growing chain of clients.

5. To spend at least a few minutes, by reading or personal contact, learning from other men in auxiliary specialized fields in order that I may provide my clients with the best guidance and service of which I am capable.

6. To devote the time needed to keep abreast of all major innovations and services as they develop in my industry and in my particular product, for I must always know the right answers for my clients. However, this must not be time taken from the precious solicitng hours of the day.

7. To keep my "light" burning for my clients. A telephone call, a note, a cup of coffee, will remind my good clients that my interest in them has not terminated with sale.

8. To make a practice of doing something to assist my fellow salesmen in appreciation for what I learn from others.

9. To keep an awareness of the need for my own financial plans to be sound.

10. To put forth an extra effort tomorrow if I have failed to accomplish any one of my goals today.

36—If You Love To Play Your Game Why Not Do It Every Day?

As a Fuller Brush man I started early in the morning to make my calls and in order to make a living I had to make at least ten to twenty sales per day. This meant talking to perhaps 25 to 50 people and ringing perhaps 100 doorbells. When I entered the life insurance business, I was told about the App-A-Week Club. This I could not understand. Why should a person spend 8 hours a day for 5 days a week and make just one sale. To me this seemed very unreasonable. I decided that in order to be happy with myself I had to sell at least one individual every day. I felt that if I made an honest effort every day for 8 hours that there would be somebody interested in my product—life insurance.

I am happy to say that over the years I have been able to maintain this effort. In fact, I was able to maintain it while running a life insurance company and a general insurance business all at the same time. I developed a formula for writing one application for life insurance for each working day from 8:30 AM to 4:30 PM. For the man who wants to work at night he can increase the number of sales he makes during these evening hours.

If it is your sincere desire to write at least one policy every working day, you can do it! Everything starts first in man's mind. Jack Wardlaw, author of several books, friend of mine for many, many years, whom I consider one of the most outstanding salesmen in the United States, expresses it best in his book entitled, *Top Secrets of Successful Selling: Thought Plus Action*. Published by Taplinger Publishing Co., New York N.Y. I recommend here that anyone who has not made a study of this book should do so, as he has covered this subject in a brilliant way.

Before acting in any way on this formula of writing a policy a day, consider the ten *"Don'ts"* below, which I find have to be followed, and which call for me to be completely brutal with the robbers of my time:

I don't read my mail;

I don't answer the telephone;

I don't run errands for my wife;

I don't give dictation or write letters;

I don't make proposals;

I don't get side-tracked by non-essentials;

I don't spend my time foolishly;

I don't let anything deter me from my goal for the day;

I don't lose my temper;

I don't have negative thoughts.

I will adhere to these *don'ts* until I have reached my goals for the day, which are to have at least one luncheon appointment for the day, a breakfast appointment for the following day, one signed application and one medical examination lined up. If possible, I like to arrange two luncheon appointments for one day. I can have an early lunch at 11:30 and a late lunch at 1:00 PM during which I will have just dessert.

To accomplish these goals requires determination, because there are continuous robbers of one's time.

When you go to your office, tell your secretary that she is to give you no phone calls until you notify her to do so. In order not to miss important calls, instruct her to let you know on a piece of paper who is on the line, just in case it is a call that could mean business. Very few people, however, will call in to buy life insurance. As a rule those persons who do call in to buy are people who are uninsurable or close to it.

Your objective is to make as many phone calls as possible now until you have your luncheon appointment, or two. When that has been accomplished, then you can relax and take the phone calls as they come as well as to call back the people who have asked you to do so.

Time is your important ingredient. There are only so many working hours in the day and there are only a certain number of hours in which you can spend time face to face with a prospect. I have made some arrangements that have been successful to serve lunch in my office. Thus I am not even wasting time in travel. If my clients object to traveling to my office, I make arrangements to have one of my secretaries pick them up.

You always have to keep in mind that you are running a business. When you do things other than selling, your store is closed. You have to be determined to spend selling time only selling. When you read your mail in the office, you are taking away selling time. I put mine in a briefcase and take it home with me and bring it back the next day. This is particularly necessary with any material which I have to study: insurance, tax publications, and so on.

By being organized in this direction, I have lots of time left for fun and recreation and charitable work. During selling time, I must keep my mind focused on one objective: to make a sale. During mealtime sessions, it is essential to hit the highlights and not to waste time on non-essentials. Follow the 1 + 1 + 1 sequence of selling, having the objective in mind to get the prospect qualified through a medical examination. Then complete the sale on another interview which again can be scheduled during a mealtime.

In the case of breakfast appointments, I have found that it is wise to have your own breakfast at your home, if possible, and reduce your intake when you are with the client to a cup of coffee or something small. Thus while the client eats, you can concentrate on the business at hand. For my luncheon appointments, I prefer to do the business first and then order the lunch. This is as true when the client comes to my office and we go out afterwards as when lunch is served in my office.

Here is what I say to myself:

Each day has as many working hours as I want to put in. Regardless of the hours, my daily objective is to write at least one application each and every working day and to deliver at least one life insurance policy to someone. My business is really not work because I enjoy every minute of it. I really have a lot of fun, and how can one call fun "work"? Some minor details I do not like to do, but I realize that not every day in your life is sunny. Occasionally it rains. And so it is with selling.

You have to shut the world off during the time you need to accomplish your objectives. And when you shut the world off, the world is yours. This applies to all salesmen who are too busy with all kinds of things but never find time to call on prospects. Unless you are able to defeat the robbers of your time day by day, you will do everything but make the necessary calls to give you the needed face-to-face exposure to make the sale you need and want. This will be an endless battle, but it has to be fought. Therefore, shut the world off for the few hours it takes, each and every working day, and your sales success is guaranteed.

37—Appointment That You Make Should Be Insured

The appointments that you make with prospects are very important to you. But to the prospect who has never met you—or to the prospect who has met you and knows you well but is reluctant to be sold—your appointment is of very minor importance. Many times it is just plain courtesy or curiosity that prompts him to agree to an appointment with you.

Since we all know the value of time—at least we all should know the value of time—it behooves each of us to use every precaution to keep appointments from being broken so that we don't find ourselves waiting for a prospect.

Many professional people charge for people who fail to arrive at the appointed time. Unfortunately, when you work on commission the time that you waste is time that never comes back. To me, time is like a sand clock. The sand is running out all the time. Each of us has only so much sand in his time clock.

We don't have the opportunity to turn the clock over at any time and let the sand start to run again. When the sand has run out, it is the end. Therefore, it is good business sense to beware of all the robbers of our time. They are not directly taking money out of our pockets, but indirectly the cost of losing time is greater than if someone actually picked our pockets. Although experience should have taught me how to prevent broken appointments, from time to time I forget that proved procedures can backfire and I find myself waiting unnecessarily for a prospect. Here is a case in point.

I had an 8:30 breakfast appointment with Jerome Snider at Rickey's restaurant which is about 15 miles away from my home. Mr. Snider had asked that we verify the appointment with his secretary the day before and that we did. I arrived at Rickey's at 8:20 and waited until 9:00 but Mr. Snider did not show up.

"Be Brutal with The Robbers of Your Time"

FORMULA
for Writing One Application Each Working Day
from 8:30 AM to 4:30 PM

The Ten Don'ts:

1. I don't read my mail.

2. I don't answer the telephone.

3. I don't run errands for my wife.

4. I don't give dictation or letters.

5. I don't make proposals.

6. I don't lose my temper.

7. I don't have negative thoughts.

8. I don't spend my time foolishly.

9. I don't get sidetracked on non-essentials.

10. I don't let anything deter me from my goal for the day.

Until These Have Been Completed:

1. Line up at least one luncheon appointment for that day (11:30 AM-1:00 PM).

2. Second appointment, if possible—1:00-2:00 PM (have dessert).

3. Line up breakfast and luncheon appointments for the rest of the week.

4. Have at least one interview every day not during mealtime.

5. While making appointments, try to set up medical examinations.

Always Keep Your Objective Clearly in Mind:

One Medical Examination Per Day.   One Delivery Per Day.

Telephone Approach:

(Ask disturbing questions to induce prospect talk)

1. When did you last purchase life insurance? What was your primary reason for buying it?
2. Do you know if you bought your insurance with taxed dollars or tax free dollars?
3. Do you know if your policies are sanforized?
4. What have you done to take inflation out of your insurance?
5. Do you have the free extras?

Learn How To Listen For Buy Signals.

If You Cannot Sell A Medical, Make An Appointment.

Don't Talk Yourself Out Of A Sale

On The Phone, Create Interest
So The Prospect Wants To See You.

Give Definite Answers Only During An Interview.

Remember:

Stick to insurance business first.

Until his check is in your hand, a prospect is only a prospect, not a client. Service is appreciated by a client, not by a prospect. When you have a client, he is entitled to service. He has paid for it. He will pay you again if you let him give you referred leads.

You are running a BUSINESS. When you are doing things other than selling, the store is CLOSED.

The cash register has to ring EVERY DAY. Keep score of the register—if you don't make a sale, put down ZERO for the day.

If you have not reached your goal during the day, put in extra effort in the evening. Have at least one sale on Saturday every week.

REMEMBER, anything you do that is not selling reduces your scale of pay to that of office clerk—if you type or act as the delivery boy, if you buy your wife's groceries, etc.

IF YOU FOLLOW THIS FORMULA RELIGIOUSLY, YOU CANNOT AVOID DOUBLING YOUR SALES.

I called his home and his wife told me that she thought that he had left for Los Angeles. Good business practice and experience had taught me in the past that although this appointment was verified, it would have been a good idea to call his home before leaving my own home. I could tell him that I might be five minutes late and not to worry because I would be there. This is good strategy and it reconfirms the appointment. Sometimes the unforeseen can crop up and a man might not be able to keep his appointment; and may not be able to reach us in order to cancel it.

If one can save ten broken appointments a year and one's closing ratio is one out of two, there are five more sales that one can make a year by avoiding broken appointments. If you make a hundred sales a year, these extra five sales mean an additional 5% of income.

Jerome Snider was an excellent prospect for me. From past conversation with him on the phone (I had never met him in person), I knew that a large amount of life insurance was needed on his wife. The fact that he broke an appointment with me created free energy for me which I used very effectively when I called him for a new appointment. On this next telephone call, I was able to convince him that before we got together for another appointment, it would be a good idea to have our medical examiner stop by his house to examine him and his wife. Jerome agreed to do that and on our final appointment the sale was consummated. Thus a problem was turned into an opportunity. The energy that I expended was not wasted. I used the energy created by his guilt feeling for not showing up for his breakfast appointment to make a bigger and better sale.

In making sure that appointments are kept, keep in mind that the fact that you call a prospect to verify an appointment does not diminish his esteem for you; on the contrary, it builds you up in his eyes because he sees that you value your time and because of this he also appreciates his own time.

If I leave my office for an appointment, it is standard procedure for my secretary to call the prospect and say something along these lines: "Mr. Bach is just about to leave the office. He will be there to see you in 15 minutes." There is no harm in using this extra precaution. When it is a luncheon appointment, my secretary will call and remind the prospect of the time and the place. Many times we will also verify an appointment with a written memorandum in addition to the telephone call.

If for any reason you find yourself in a place without a prospect because he has failed to keep his appointment, don't dismay. This gives you an opportunity to meet the owner or the manager. He has not heard your story and if you are willing to talk to a few people on a cold canvass basis, you will find that your time does not necessarily have to be completely wasted.

Mealtime has become one of the most valuable periods for me. By spending breakfast, lunch or dinner or having coffee or a drink with a possible client, I make good use of this time. Even the busiest prospect cannot deny that he has to take time out to eat.

38—How To Increase Your Volume With Very Little Effort

Most people do not own enough life insurance and when they are about to buy life insurance they do not think in large amounts. If you talk about too large an amount of insurance in a sales interview, a ready customer will often refuse to buy without telling you why. What has happened is that he has become frightened by the amount of life insurance you suggested. It is very important that you present your proposition in such a way as not to frighten the prospect. The very same person who becomes scared about the size of a policy thinks nothing, however, of a large accidental death policy.

In my opinion, accidental death insurance has no place in the program of the client because it only rewards the cause of death. If a certain amount of insurance protection is needed we cannot speculate on the cause of death. However, we cannot eliminate human nature, and free energy applied simply means to use the free energy created by the prospect in situations of this type.

Over the years, I have used a simple system which has been very successful. I merely apply for an alternate policy or two for double or triple the original amount. This simple procedure has been instrumental in selling millions of dollars of additional insurance. I have also had great success with the use of a term rider for the original amount of the policy or double the amount of the policy originally applied for. I simply call this rider an all-purpose double indemnity rider. Instead of' paying double in the event of accidental death only, it pays double in the event of any death. Here is an example:

You have just placed a $10,000 policy on Mr. Jones with double indemnity. You say to him, "Mr. Jones, I am not sure if I told you that you are also entitled to the all-purpose type of double indemnity. In fact, if you wish, you are entitled to add an all-purpose triple indemnity rider. Let me show you how we can do this. The all-purpose double indemnity pays double in any kind of death, whereas a normal double indemnity clause pays double only in the event of an accidental death, and contains a whole variety of exclusions. The all-purpose double indemnity has no exclusions whatsoever."

Having added these so-called term riders to a basic policy, you not only increase your volume decisively, but at the same time you open the door for future trade-in's of the term portions without medical examinations. In my opinion this simple tool should be used by every salesman. This idea is not original with me. But like so many outstanding ideas, many of us use them for a certain period of time and then discard them and seek to find new and better ideas.

In more than a quarter of a century of life insurance selling, I have not found a better vehicle to double my production than the alternate all-purpose double or triple indemnity clause. I recommend here that you make a list of the various ideas you are now successfully using—a checklist of some sort. Then from time to time go over the list and see if you are still using techniques that have been important to you in the past. For most salesmen, there often develops a period of poor production. This is called a sales slump. In checking why we are in this slump, we often find that it was created by the omission of some simple ideas that have proved in the past to be excellent, but which the salesman for no reason at all has disregarded. All that is needed to get out of the sales slump is to re-adopt the old fundamentals.

Another valuable sales idea that has been responsible for much business is a letter that our underwriting department sends with a policy when the underwriter feels that the amount of insurance applied for is not enough, based on the information he has about the prospect's finances. Such a letter can be a tremendously valuable sales tool.

San Francisco Life *Insurance Company*

160 Sansome Street, San Francisco, California 94104   (415) 981-2760
Teletype 910-372-6069

We are very pleased to inform you that your client has qualified as an
outstanding risk for our company. From every standpoint; medical, moral
and financial, he falls into a group that the company is proud to insure.

Because of this he will be entitled to the additional amount of protection, as mentioned below, provided there have been no unforeseen changes
in his health or occupation. To obtain the additional protection the
first premium payment (whether annual, semi-annual, quarterly, or monthly)
must be made before the date that the option expires. A signed application for the additional policy is to accompany the payment.

                    Sincerely,

                    Richard A. Larson
                    Assistant Secretary
                    Chief Underwriter

This offer in the amount of $_____ expires_____.

With a satisfactory statement of health this offer is extended to

_____.

89

39—How To Write Bigger Cases: The Desire Of Most Life Insurance Agents

The desire of every salesman in the country to increase his earnings prompts this question. If a life insurance salesman averages $300 per policy and he writes 50 policies per year, his annual premium income is $15,000. If he can write 100 policies, naturally his premium income will be double and if he can write 150 policies, it will be triple. So one way to increase one's production is to be more efficient and to write more sales with the same type of prospect.

The other way to up your income is to write the same number of lives but prospect in a market where the average premium is much higher. All of these things are much easier said than done. Speaking from my own experience and the experiences of others whose careers I have followed, I can only say that a combination of the two is better than just trying to go for the bigger cases.

In looking back over my business life in the life insurance industry, I have found that I always needed a lot of activity. To me making a sale, regardless of how small it was, was a new inspiration. I was able to open up a new account with someone and build a clientele which, if I would service it well, would eventually grow with me.

My desire from the very beginning has always been to make as many sales as possible. If a day would go by without a sale, I would be very unhappy because I felt that I had accomplished nothing. I sincerely believe that the standards in that respect in the life insurance business, standards set by sales managers and the companies themselves, over the years have been way too low. Most companies have an app-a-week club, which means that a man becomes a hero if he gets one application a week. If he gets one application a week, that does not mean that he is going to place 52 policies in one year, because not every policy will be issued and not every policy will be accepted by the prospect.

I would like to advocate for the industry a new standard—a standard of writing an application a day. It has always been my opinion that if we put in an eight hour day of honest solicitation and effort into helping people to die for all they are worth, then our results should at least produce one new client per day.

I feel that if more emphasis were to be put on the development of salesmen who will open accounts rather than on the development of salesmen who look at big volume, the business of life insurance would be better off and the people of the United States would be better off because of the additional coverage that would protect their families.

In looking back over the years, I find that I average about the same number of open accounts per year from one year to the next with very little variation, including the first year. This number has always been over the 200 mark which means paying for approximately one case per day. This indicates, however, that my selling skill had to improve because in the early years, very little of my time was spent on service work. I was establishing a new business and I had no old clients that needed my attention. Today a lot of my time is dedicated to service of the old policyholder who had hired me for this service when he bought from me. Let me come back to service later, because service can mean a lot of different things to different people.

In my younger years also I was able to spend more hours in selling. I know that for many years I came home at 11:00 or 12:00 at night five nights a week, because I would never stop until I had my sale for the day.

I also know that I was not a natural born salesman and that I did not have the natural talents to be successful. In fact, I flunked the aptitude test. The reason I know this is that the company did not want to give me an advance of any form. They graciously agreed to let me work on commission only.

This observation also proves to me that skill and talents can be developed by working on it continuously. One of my mother's cousins was married to the famous violinist, Mischa Elman. Mr. Elman used to visit during the summertime in the town of Atherton where I live, and I was amazed when I learned that this world famous violinist, who was endowed with all of nature's talents, would practice his violin every day for six hours.

This in itself could be a very valuable lesson for every salesman. In order to increase one's income and selling skill with it, or the reverse thereof, it is essential that we learn how to improve ourselves; that we learn how to improve our knowledge of our business and related subjects at all times; and that we revise our goals upward continuously and work on them without let-up.

All of this is easier said than done. I believe that with the increase of one's sales ability, and sales knowledge, there has to come an increase in the growth of the man. Our prospects sense the quality of the man with whom they deal. They sense if one is sincere or insincere. They sense if one has a real desire to be of service or if one is interested only in making a commission. They feel it when they are dealing with a hit and run salesman.

One of the best tools of free energy, in my humble opinion, is sincerity. To have the real desire to help the other fellow in one's heart does not cost anything, but that real desire, that intent to improve the other man's position, is powerful energy. It is wireless submitted energy that radiates your surroundings. It is energy that builds your reputation and, although reputation does not have a market value per se, its value to a salesman is immeasurable. But what can increase the salesman's income? What concrete ways are there? The most important one of all is prospecting upwards.

Unfortunately, in this economic world, when it comes to business, everything is measured in dollars and cents. By prospecting upwards, you have to set your goals to develop gradually a type of prospect whose income is larger than that of your previous prospects.

With more income comes more ability to save larger sums of money. Therefore, it stands to reason that if you change your mode of prospecting to people with higher incomes, your average size case should be larger.

How can one prospect upwards? This is very simple. You have to decide to change your market and become more or less a specialist in certain income fields or groups. For instance, working with a professional market will automatically put you in a higher income group. This group can include physicians, dentists, attorneys, pharmacists, veterinarians, architects and engineers. And naturally the business market will also give you the same opportunity.

I have met many men over the years who have specialized in one profession only, such as the physicians market. Their production has always been way above the average. I personally have never felt that I wanted to be a specialist in any one field. However, I have always felt that I want to be a specialist for every prospect with whom I am working at a particular time, by giving my very best to his situation; and when it is warranted, I will call in an outside specialist to provide the knowledge and the services that I can not perform.

With many men with whom I have worked and given this advice, I found that it did not work; and in checking through with them, I learned that they just did not change their old habits; they continued doing what they had been doing right along. It was easier for them to seek bigger and greener pastures, but they did not have the guts to do the job. It is easy to tell but it's hard to do.

Yes, it is not easy suddenly to call on people with whom you do not feel as comfortable; with whom you do not feel as much at ease. Like some salesmen, you might feel inferior. I do not believe that any man is inferior to another because of less education or a lower financial situation. Furthermore, I learned that the bigger the man, the easier he was to deal with once I got to him.

Concerning the desire to prospect upwards, we have to remember that we will change ourselves only gradually. It will take time for us to feel at ease with this new type of prospect, but this feeling will come very quickly when we make some sales to him; and before long we will have reached a new plateau from which the next climb to greater accomplishment will come.

40—Using Free Energy To Increase Your Sales

John Lash had applied for $100,000 worth of life insurance. He went through his medical examination and almost three weeks passed by and still the underwriting results of his application did not come in. I received a call from John inquiring about the status of his application. I assured him that there was no reason for him to worry, that somehow a delay on his application could have been caused by a vacationing physician's report not being completed—things like that happen all the time.

It took a total of five weeks to get the final approval and John Lash qualified as a perfect risk for this $100,000 policy. I immediately decided to use his anxiety to my advantage and called the underwriter to get approval on the maximum amount of insurance for which his examination had qualified him. In this instance, the underwriter was willing to approve another $50,000 worth of life insurance.

Fortified with this new ammunition, I went to see John Lash. I collected the premiums not on the $100,000 he had bought but on $150,000 that I had decided he probably would accept. It took no more energy to place this $150,000 than it would have taken to place the $100,000, but if I can repeat this technique twelve times a year, I will increase my production by $600,000. That is why at all times, day in and day out, I live by the principle "a problem becomes an opportunity." And there are many opportunities where this sort of situation creates sales for me that otherwise could not be made.

Let me give another example: I received a telephone call from Armond Wilson, who operates a very successful business on the San Francisco peninsula. He has a partner who was the toughest man I ever had to sell. They had been clients of mine for some time. I had been instructed to work with their attorney to see that their partnership insurance was integrated into a buy-and-sell agreement. I had no control over the service that their attorney was going to give them. Almost two years passed and the attorney did not complete his work.

Armond complained that I was the one who should be able to get his attorney to do his job. Rather than react to his complaint in a negative fashion, I decided to build on it. I said, "Armond, your attorney is a very wise man because he has probably seen businesses like yours whose characters changed perhaps in a short period of time. Maybe your business is just like that. Have you had any growth in the last two years?"

Armond said, "Well, I wouldn't sell my business today for twice what it was worth two years ago."

I said, "Armond, since that is the case, we had better thank the attorney for having been slow because I have been guilty of not bringing the value of your insurance protection up to its present level. And I had better take care of that right now and make sure that the agreement that your attorney is drawing up will be in line with present values."

This telephone conversation resulted in a beautiful additional amount of production—again turning a problem into an opportunity.

Another example: An incorporated group of veterinarians had their life insurance with me, and the corporation's premium came due but the check did not arrive. A day before the expiration of their contracts, I decided to get on the telephone to find out what the problem was. The individual who answered the phone was Dr. Wally Henderson, and he was not one of the clients I had insured. In my telephone conversation I discovered that he was a new man joining the group of veterinarians and, as a result of this service call, Dr. Henderson will be added to the list of clients, the lifeblood of my business.

I cannot help adding another interesting example dealing with a similar situation. One of my secretaries decided to stay home and be a housekeeper for a while, but after a few months of staying at home she decided to go back to work. I received a call from her new employer asking me about her qualifications. Since she was one of the most outstanding secretaries I have ever had, I could only be very enthusiastic in my references for her.

I immediately turned this time into selling time by asking her new employer if he knew the type of business I was in. He said he did. I told him I was very glad he did because, since we had this opportunity to meet each other over the phone, I wanted to make sure that I would get to know him in person and to get him acquainted with the outstanding products that we have available. He turned out to be an excellent prospect and is now a client. This one telephone call will also result in a very substantial amount of additional life insurance for other associates of this client.

Daily interruptions of this nature, which could have taken away a lot of business time, have actually resulted in a vast amount of business on people with whom I had never planned to deal. In all of these instances, I have kept my sales story simple because I wanted these people to be buyers as quickly as possible. In all instances, I assumed that the value of my product had already been previously sold by others; that the prospect was intelligent enough to realize the value of my product; and that by giving him an easy opportunity to make the purchase, he would find the money to pay for it.

Again, with the use of my simple question and answer system, I was able to establish in a very few moments the likes and the dislikes of the prospect, his feelings, for his family and his ambitions for himself.

I cannot overemphasize that if he masters this technique, any salesman can double or triple his production; but I must also emphasize that this is a process which does not work at once. You have to develop it, practice it and give it a chance to become part of your own operation. One other very important point: you cannot expect results unless you have brakes on your tongue. You do have to learn to listen and you have to be able to keep your mouth shut long enough for the prospect to do the talking.

Another way to get additional business is to call a prospect between two and four weeks after he has purchased life insurance. My conversation generally goes as follows:

"Mr. Prospect, the reason for my call is to find out if there is anything that I have promised to do for you that I might have forgotten. Also, is there anything that you feel I can do for you in connection with your whole program that I might have overlooked?"

I wait for the answer and then I proceed:

"I would like to know for my records, Mr. Prospect, what was your most motivating reason for purchasing the life insurance you did from me?"

I wait for his answer and I say:

"If I could get you an additional $25,000 at this time, would that interest you? I have this amount available to you without further medical examination."

In many instances this telephone call results in additional business.

Now in order to build an endless chain of prospects, I continue with the following practical question, "Mr. Prospect, I am quite sure that you have discussed your purchase of life insurance with some of your friends or neighbors. Who do you feel would derive the most benefit from my services?"

I wait for the answer and very often I get some rewarding leads. It is essential that you keep a record of the reason your prospect bought his life insurance. It should be in your files because many times in the future you might have to re-sell the need for his protection, and when you know why he bought it in the first place, you can motivate him easier to retaining it.

41—Getting By The Secretary

Much of my time is spent on the telephone setting up appointments with people I have never met before. In attempting to secure such appointments I have, over the years, run across many efficient secretaries. Often it is impossible to get over this hurdle. I frequently receive this objection from a faithful secretary:

"Will you please tell me the nature of your business and the name of your company?"

The secretary has been instructed to screen for her boss all intruders that can take away his valuable time. When I get this kind of question, I say:

"You know, you are like my own secretary. You really protect your boss, don't you? My secretary has been instructed on the same lines and I appreciate you very much. Will you tell your boss that Mr. Bach is on the line and he wants to talk to him about a personal matter?"

If she resists further, I say, "Can I have your name, please, for my files?" On a future call, I address her by first name and succeed more readily.

When the prospect comes on the phone, I congratulate him immediately on his efficient secretary. And I say:

"Your secretary asked me what my business is and I told her my call was of a personal nature. I would like to clarify that for you. I am in the life insurance business. Possibly the last person you want to talk to is another life insurance man. Is that correct? However, Mr. Prospect, I am a little different from the average life insurance salesman. I have an idea that I believe could be of value to you and unless I can give it to you, you might never hear about it."

Here is where my skill and persistence are brought to bear in order to sell a favorable appointment. Most prospects will ask: "Well, what is your idea?"

I then say: "Mr. Prospect, since you are a very busy man, you probably have not had a chance to take the inflation out of the life insurance you now own and to get an up-to-date performance record on your life insurance. Is that correct?"

Usually the prospect will want to know what I mean. In that case, I simply say:

"I do not want to insult your intelligence by going into an important matter like this over the telephone. The reason for my call, Mr. Prospect, is to find out when we can spend a few minutes together in order to explain this important idea to you."

Many of my calls are not productive, but I always keep in mind that beyond the call on which I do not succeed lies the call on which I will succeed. Naturally, the success of any given call depends upon the preparation that goes into the call before I make it. If the call is a referred lead, my chances of getting by the secretary and getting an appointment are much greater. The important thing is to keep on playing the game of selling at all times with the same energy, with the same spirit of enthusiasm, and it will be fun.

42—Free Energy In Your Prospect's Objections

Securities And Insecurities

Quite often, a prospect will tell you that he is interested only in the stock market or other equity investments. If you find yourself in this situation, try the following to awaken him to the difference between life insurance and other investments:

"Mr. Prospect, when you purchase a security, who carries the risk? . . ." (WAIT FOR AN ANSWER)

"Is it the stock brokerage firm, or is it you? . . .

"Is there any doubt in your mind that the entire risk is held by you? . . .

"In contrast, when you purchase life insurance, who carries the risk? . . .

"Unreservedly, is it you or is it the life insurance company? . . .

"Is there any question in your mind that it is the life insurance company? . . .

"Is it the business of the life insurance company to carry risks? . . . And because it is the insurance company's business to carry risks, there are strict regulations requiring an insurance company to carry large reserves to meet unexpected losses, which would otherwise be ruinous to you.

"Can you afford to carry these large reserves and be in the risk business? What is the true difference between the stockbroker and the life insurance salesman? Has it ever occurred to you that the stockbroker deals in 'insecurities' and the life insurance agent deals in 'real securities'?

"One other thought: When you look in the newspaper six months from now, you don't know what the value of the stockbroker's security will be worth, but I can show you the value of a life insurance security on the dot, year by year, month by month, as many years ahead as you wish. You can have instant cash, come what may."

Then I show how life insurance works by using my favorite ledger salestalk.

43—On Closing

There Is No Sense In Opening A Sales Interview Unless You Are Willing To Perfect Your Closing Technique

You have to study your closes repeatedly and you have to remember them. Use them again and again until they become as natural to you as breathing. One thing to bear in mind: no one can teach you when to close. You learn when to close only by closing too early too often. You will never learn when to close if you continue to close too seldom and too late. Many times it is wise to prepare for a close by using a story. Never forget stories in this business—good hard-hitting stories. Here is a story about Benjamin Franklin.

"We Americans have long considered Ben Franklin one of our wisest men. Whenever Ben found himself faced with making a decision in a situation such as the one you are in today, Mr. Prospect, he felt fairly much as you do. If it were the right thing to do, he wanted to be sure to do it. If it were the wrong thing, he wanted to be sure to avoid it. Isn't that about the way you feel, Mr. Prospect? He would take a sheet of plain paper and draw a line down the center. On one side of the line he would write the word 'Yes', and on the other side he would write the word 'No'. Under the 'Yes' he would list all the favorable aspects, and under the 'No' he would list the negative aspects. When he was through he simply counted the reasons in each column and he decided accordingly."

By the way, you will find the Ben Franklin story in *Poor Richard's Almanac*. The Ben Franklin story is a honey for the indecisive prospect.

The "I'll Think It Over" Close

When a man says anything to you that resembles the "I'll think it over" objection, you can answer along these lines.

"That is fine. Obviously, you wouldn't take your time thinking it over, Mr. Prospect, unless you were really interested, would you? And I am sure that you are not telling me this just to get rid of me. May I assume that you will give it very careful consideration?"

By this time the prospect will think you are going to let him get away. He will agree with you. He will say, "yes, I'll give it careful consideration," or "I will really think about it." Now he is agreeing with you, so you continue:

"What specific point about this proposal is it that you wish to think over? Is it a question of the benefits you will receive? Is it this? Is it that? . . . " until you have covered all the points you made in your sales presentation. Soon your prospect will grab one of your questions and he will answer: "Yes, that's what I want to think over."

What does this give you? You are being handed a final objection and you can close now on that final objection.

Here is one important point to remember in this close. If you stop for a breath *at the crucial point*, you jeopardize your entire tactic. It is when you ask, "Which point do you wish to think over?" that you must not stop for breath. If you stop for breath, the prospect will say, "The whole thing," and it will all be over for you. You must get into the first, "Is it . . .?" without the slightest pause. This will work.

The problem of "I'll think it over" is that it never gives you an objection to fight. It is too intangible. By using this close, you will reduce the intangibility of "I'll think it over" to the tangibility of an objection that you are competent to handle.

Of course, there are times, legitimate times, when the prospect really means what he says with the "I'll think it over" objection and when he asks you to call him back. But never on a call back to the prospect should you ask, "Have you thought it over?" because the prospect will say, "Yes, I have, and the answer is no."

The prospect rarely thinks it over in your favor. He forgets you and all positive points in your proposition five minutes after you have left him. The only things he remembers about your sales presentation are the negatives. The most successful way to come back on your next interview with him is to say, "Mr. Prospect, I must apologize to you. There was something that I forgot to show you the last time we got together."

You have to arouse a new interest and then go over your entire sales proposition again. You have to make this proposition better than the first one, but be sure to add some new and useful information.

The Yes Closing

The most critically important and fundamental instruction in the field of closing is this: after you ask a closing question, KEEP QUIET, KEEP QUIET, and KEEP QUIET. The first man to talk loses the game. When you ask a closing question, KEEP QUIET. If you keep quiet, one of two things happens: either he goes along with you or he will give you a reason for not going along with you. As a salesman you can cash in on either one. After three seconds of silence you may become nervous, but KEEP QUIET. There is no pressure you can exert that will ever remotely approach the pressure of silence.

I do not care how long you sit still. If you have to sit for twenty minutes, the two words KEEP QUIET are still the most important words you will have to learn. Silence can hit hard. Be silent the way a high energy wire is silent. Then get your free energy salesmanship working for you by throwing the switch.

Free Energy Closing Techniques

(The following sample techniques have been very successful, especially with tough prospects)
1.   "Mr. Prospect, I am delighted to tell you that I have a number for you which can be worth a lot of money. Would you please write down number 30,050 on this piece of paper. This number, Mr. Prospect, can be worth $100,000 the minute it is written on your check in the amount of $100 made payable to San Francisco Life Insurance Company." In closing a case with a prospect who offers you tough resistance and who says he wants to think it over, the following has been successful:

2.   "Mr. Prospect, do you have a piece of paper? Would you please write down this number —30,050. This is the

number for the insurance for which you have qualified. After you have thought it over and you decide you want this protection, make out your check for $2,000 and be sure to put this number—30,050—on it. If you will mail this check to me, we will put the insurance company on the risk right now. "You might want to think it over and still be covered in the meantime. In that case, all we will need is $200 (one-tenth of the annual premium) and that will cover you for the next 60 days. Be sure to write the number 30,050 on your check and you will have the coverage for 60 days. After you have decided you want it we will then bill you for the balance of the annual premium." Another approach similar to the above two which is also useful to counteract the prospect's objection that he wants to think it over is the following:

3. "Mr. Prospect, do you have a blank check with you? Would you please write this number on the check. (Give number of policy.) After you and your wife have thought it over you can put this check in the mail and we will cover you. The check will be good for at least 60 days of protection. You have now transferred the risk from yourself to us. However, you may want to do better than this. Many times we are prevented from doing what we want to do. You can let me hold your check now and if I don't hear from you within the next three days then we will put it through and that way you don't have to call me. Would that be all right?" In many situations, the prospect will let you do this, but you will never know until you give it a chance.

Half Of Something Is Better Than All Of Nothing

Many times I cannot get a decision from a prospect on the amount of insurance he would like to have. In such a situation, rather than wait for a decision at a later date, I try to settle then and there, even for the smallest amount, and try to leave the prospect with the idea that I will be back to give him the amount that he really needs and wants to have sometime in the future. The reason for this thinking is that once I have made a client of my prospect, it is easier for me to come back to him *as a client* than as a prospect whom I did not sell. It is easier to build on something that you have created than on something that has never been accomplished. I always like to talk in units. If a man buys a $25,000 policy from me, I consider it a quarter of a unit. If he buys $50,000 it is half a unit. And I always leave him with this idea in mind: *I will be back to complete the unit.* Now to the really big corporate buyer, a unit will be a one million dollar policy, and so on. Just the other day, I called one of my corporate clients who, unfortunately, could afford only $50,000 of coverage on each of his three key people including himself. I waited only six months from the date of his original purchase to call him back. I said, "Ray, this is Karl Bach. I am calling regarding your key man coverage. In the past you bought only half a unit. The purpose of my call today is to make sure that you will have a full unit at this time." He said, "Karl, go ahead. It is a good idea."

Assumed consent is full of free energy. Use it often, but give the prospect a chance to stop you.

Determination In Closing

When you are ready to close a sales situation, I know from experience you have to give it all you have. You can be agreeable with your prospect throughout the entire sales presentation, but when it comes to the final close, you have to be determined to get your way. You will lose free energy by being nice and letting the prospect determine that you will see him again, that he is going to think the proposition over, or letting him give you one of the millions of excuses that arise when people are indecisive. This will only make your work more difficult—in fact, an almost impossible task. If you can train yourself to be tough with the close, your sales will increase substantially. The case of Anthony Peterson illustrates this well.

Anthony Peterson is a big fruit grower in San Jose and was recommended to me as a good prospect by another client. I could never reach Anthony on the phone, so I made a cold canvass call at his business one day and was lucky to find him in and in a receptive mood.

Surely he would like to talk about life insurance, but there was no need to get my ideas, he told me. He had $200,000 policy on the desk in front of him. As a matter of fact he had just received it. I asked him if the policy were in force. Anthony said *no*, that the agent who had written the policy tried to get the money but he had wanted to think about it and that the agent had him sign a letter which stated that the policy was left only for inspection and that the insurance was not in force. This, incidentally, is the form most companies insist that their agents use when they leave a policy without premium payment.

Here is where my free energy started to work. I said, "Anthony, how would you like to have a piece of paper that says $200,000 is in force and payable right now?"

He asked me how I could do it. I said, "First let me give you the plan that I have in mind and if you like my prescription then you can give me your check and we will have you covered right away."

"I could have done that with the other agent."

"Yes, but you didn't and I want to make sure that you have a contract of insurance that is in force."

After consulting at length with Anthony Peterson about his financial objectives, I wrote him a $300,000 policy and got a check for the first quarterly premium. I later took him to the doctor. He qualified on all the medicals and the business was placed.

The competing agent was a man well-known to me and one of the Bay Area's most outstanding life insurance underwriters. As it happened, we met at a later date and we discussed this case. He wanted to know why he had lost it. I explained to him that had he tried a little harder to get the check when he had left the policy for inspection, I would have been completely out in the cold and would have had no chance to make a client of Anthony Peterson.

44—"I Am Not Interested In Life Insurance . . ."

Many books have been written on the subject of life insurance and life insurance salesmen. The picture of life insurance salesmen painted in many such books is unfavorable: salesmen are envisioned as "something to get rid of." I believe all the objections raised against life insurance salesmen can be overcome with the right answers.

Before, however, we proceed to meet the objections of our prospects, we must first have the proper conviction of our product in our hearts and the purpose of our prospects first in our minds. Once these priorities are deeply engrained in our thinking, our answers, whatever they might be, will bring with them the extra power to create sufficient free energy to turn a prospect into a client.

When the prospect says, "I am not interested in life insurance," he is actually making a statement which, if properly explained, he would be hard put to substantiate. If he is working for a living, he is interested in life insurance, because he is making money and probably trying to save some of it. He is in fact not at present abandoning his family and letting his children starve because he is not interested in money. He is interested in money, and, in the last analysis, life insurance is also money. There is no man in the world who can say he has enough money.

Naturally, there are some men who are young and retired, but in most instances, even the richest men want to acquire more money for whatever reasons they have to acquire it. I would like to repeat here what I have previously stated so often: Life insurance is a *monopoly*. Life insurance is the only product in the world for which there is no substitute. Life insurance is the only product that has no competition. Therefore, if we are completely convinced of the value of our product, and the value of the mission of life insurance (some people even call it the religion of life insurance), then, whatever the objections to a sales proposition, we are fortified, equipped and able to channel the objection into a positive reason for the purchase of life insurance.

45—Free Energy And Human Nature

Never get trapped with comparisons and figures. Some of the dearest lessons that I have had to learn in my career have come from so-called cost comparisons. Most of the time, if a prospect is comparing the cost of life insurance, we assume that he is ready to buy and that all he is trying to do now is to buy the best life insurance contract for the best price to suit his situation. Don't get trapped by making a comparison with figures.

The best way to avoid this trap is to stick to selling ideas and concepts. However, there are exceptions to every rule. When you let the prospect make his own comparisons you are minimizing your own chances of getting the sale. You are reducing your chances to a very small percentage because the decision is being made without your presence. You have no way of controlling the outcome of the sale. The figures left by your competitors could show all kinds of factors that your presentation does not contain.

I am sure you are all familiar, for example, with the variations of dividend projections. Your proposition could contain the valuable disability waiver, disability income or double indemnity, whereas your competitor's proposal might not include these benefits. And if you assume that the prospect has learned enough about the insurance business to make a correct comparison, you will pay dearly for this assumption.

Regardless of how many years we have spent in our business, there are always new things we can learn. The prospect, his controller, his accountant or his attorney, are not equipped to be expert buyers of life insurance. Therefore, if you get trapped into a cost comparison, observe the most important rule: be sure that you are on hand when the comparison is being made. If you have to be on hand *even* with your competitor when the comparison is being made, be there. However, if you are wise, you will avoid getting trapped into a situation like this because life insurance is never bought based on figures alone. Life insurance is bought with ideas, motivation and the desire to protect one's family and one's business.

One of my standard ways of getting action when the matter of figures arises has been to insist on getting the figures exactly and permanently. The only way I can obtain these figures is by having the prospect submit himself to a medical examination. In most cases, if I am able to make the sale of the medical examination, my chances of getting the business in a final sale will be increased tremendously.

Most of my competitors take the easy way out and furnish figures and proposals without a guarantee that they can deliver. If the prospect has submitted himself to a medical examination for me, the chances that he will do so again for someone else are remote. If a large amount of life insurance is involved, I get all the necessary tests, such as electrocardiogram and Master's test as well as x-ray. I can assure you that very few prospects will do this for two agents at the same time.

Jerome Breyer, my mentor, taught me this procedure. I will always remember his words to the prospect. "When we get the figures back from the insurance company, Mr. Prospect, then you will compare my figures with my competitor's and you will put two and two together. If our figures are better, no doubt we will have earned the right to your business. If we are equal, then you can take your choice either to split the business or award it to whomever you believe is entitled to it. If we are not as competitive, it is obvious that we cannot expect the right to your business. Is that fair enough?"

Over the years this lesson has proved itself over and over again. It is a lesson, however, that I have to re-learn from time to time because like so many things that I know are working for me I may put them aside and try new ideas simply because I get tired of the old ones. But we are wasting our energy if we are trying to improve on something that is as perfect as it can be.

Another rule it pays to follow is: Remember always, never compete by comparing the same plan of insurance. There are usually too many variable factors to make the comparison exact and fair. Better present another plan that your competitor does not have and sell its good points and the close. The important point is to put your product into the hands of the prospect. That is your goal and objective.

When I think of selling concepts, I cannot help remembering a very large case which resulted in my getting one of the best clients I have. I did not expect competition when I arrived at the prospect's office, but the first thing he said was that he wanted to have my figures, that he had been checking with another company. He even gave me the name of the other company, and I knew at once that I had tough competition.

The following discussion developed:

"Mr. Prospect, I could compare figures with you and you will find that we might be better during a certain period of the contract than the competition. During another period of the contract, however, the competition might be better than we are. But I believe I can best answer your questions when we look at the total concept of what you are trying to accomplish.

"My competition has offered you a short term contract with options to renew. I am recommending the longest contract possible—a contract that lasts for life. I believe, and you probably will agree with me, that no one has a lease on life, but if you should live, it is my feeling that the amount of insurance we talk about today will be inadequate ten to twenty years from now. We know your financial situation today; but we can only guess about the future."

As a consequence of my talking in this manner in general terms, the client closed the case with me that day. I attribute this to the fact that I dealt in broad concepts rather than specifics. By explaining to him that a whole life contract is nothing but a life term contract, and that the actuaries who design the insurance contracts have to use basic assumptions, I made the point with him that he could never make a mistake, regardless of which contract he was going to purchase.

46—Even Your Competitor Provides Free Energy

How To Handle Competition:

It generally pays to avoid competition altogether. Competition is putting life insurance on a par with a commodity. Service is not and should not be a matter of barter. Service cannot be weighed and a price fixed accordingly. An attorney with many years of experience might charge much more for an hour of his time than a young attorney with no experience. Service is a matter of confidence, knowledge and judgment.

If your prospect asks about another company, it is always wise to praise the other company. If a prospect talks about another agent, it is always wise to say something nice about him. It never pays to knock the competition. Frequently you hear, "I have a friend in the business." My answer to this is usually, "Mr. Prospect, I am not selling friendship, but I am selling a service and ideas and I know that you do not want to take away something from someone that belongs to him." It is never wise to allow competition to come into the sales process. It is wise to avoid it. But one has to be prepared to meet it.

The following rules regarding competition will pay off:

1.   Never knock any other company when talking to a prospect.

2.   Never knock any other salesman.

3.   Never knock anybody or anything. This is a good rule to use throughout your life.

4. Instead of comparing policy contracts, change to a different plan and present your own ideas rather than the ideas that your competitor introduced.

The following statement has been very powerful when competition has entered the picture:

"Mr. Prospect, with my contract comes an additional ingredient that is not contained in writing. It is my ability and my desire to be of service to you as long as I live. To the best of my ability, I will make sure that your insurance is in force at all times. My office staff and I will be working for you throughout the lifetime of your contract."

And then I quote an example: A few months ago, a new client of mine who had bought a substantial life insurance policy which was paid on a monthly basis went to Europe. While in Europe, he developed a serious illness. He had to be hospitalized over there and his wife went to Europe to stay with him during his illness. Naturally, no one in the family thought of the life insurance premiums which had to be paid. His premium came due. I had no way of getting in contact with the prospect or his family. But I knew that he was seriously ill and would want this insurance to stay in force. I decided to pay his premium for him, anticipating that I would be able to collect as soon as I heard from the prospect.

As it turned out, two of his other policies that he had purchased from another agent lapsed and because of his illness and medical history, he could not qualify for reinstatement. Nor will he ever be able to qualify again. Because of my little extra service and effort a large amount of life insurance, bought from me, is now giving him extra peace of mind. His illness is incurable.

PART V

Selling With The Help Of Others

47—Two Brains Know More Than One—The Case Clinic

You have called on the prospect, Mr. Jones, two or three times, and each time you have been unable to assist him in buying your product. Each time you have failed to make him understand the necessary factors. Each time you have failed to create the desire for your product. That is why you have been unable to create business. However, you still feel that you have a prospect. You still feel, and rightfully so, that perhaps the next time around you will receive a decision.

This could or could not be so. In such a situation, your case could be discussed with one of your associates whose judgment you respect or in a case clinic with several of your associates. I often am amazed how successful just such a procedure has been for me in placing far more life insurance than I had originally intended.

The case clinic offers you the advantages of the thinking of other persons who will look at your prospect's financial picture from a new light and view it with an open mind. Your colleagues will not have received any preconceived notions of the prospect's likes and dislikes. In addition, the case clinic enables you to view the entire case anew yourself.

In most instances, the agent who has not succeeded could have been successful if from the beginning, he had applied the principles of free energy by the use of selected questioning and a longer listening period, as well as careful study of the chapter in my book, *How I Sell $12,000,000 of Life Insurance Year after Year*, entitled "Seven Words That Can Protect You From Failure." (See excerpt in the Appendix.)

In most instances where the salesman's first efforts have met with unfavorable results, he would be wise to begin thinking of introducing a new face, a specialist. Instead of selling his product at the moment, the agent should start selling his specialist. This specialist, with the proper build-up and only with the proper build-up, can often effect the sale where the original agent has failed. This does not detract from the original salesman. On the contrary, it gives him support. Frequently, it is merely a face-saving device for the prospect who, having said no, even after he has been convinced, will persevere in his negative reaction because personal pride will not permit him to reveal his initial lack of good judgment.

Through the agent's elicitation of the help of a third party, the prospect has the opportunity to reply as he truly wishes. The psychological factors entering into such a decision can probably be well documented by a psychologist, but the important thing is that we are giving the required help to our prospect in buying the product of life insurance, for which there is no substitute.

Once again I would like to state that life insurance is a monopoly. No other product can provide its service. This is something that we continuously must keep in mind, because the knowledge of it could create a wealth of free energy and generative power.

48—How To Make More Sales By Calling In The Expert

Using an expert or calling in a pinch-hitter before you lose a sale can help your growth in the life insurance business tremendously. The fact that I did so throughout my career has probably made me. Yes, I have learned from the pro's. We have the practice of splitting commissions from such joint work and, actually, a split commission in such a situation is like a gift from heaven. The expert gets paid, not by what you do for him, but by what he does for you; and you get paid while you watch him at work. You receive the benefits of his many years of experience.

John Leipsic, CLU, is a young but very successful life insurance professional in San Francisco. Because John's father, a prominent attorney, was one of my clients and died very young, I was always interested in John's career in the life insurance business. Here John is speaking for himself concerning the benefits that so-called joint work brings him.

There are times when we go through all the motions of making a sale but for some unknown reason, we "strike out" at the plate. When I am faced with this predicament, I turn to a "pinch hitter" to see if he can drive home the run and make the sale for me. These cases were closed by "pinch hitters" after I had struck out with the bases loaded.

First, let me mention how I use the "team" method of calling in a "pinch hitter." My company has a weekly "case clinic" program during which agents (team members) are encouraged to present various case situations which are causing them difficulty or seem impossible to close. In most instances, the insurance has already been approved. The clinics are chaired by one of a group of multi-million dollar producers known throughout the life insurance industry, such as Karl Bach, Ed Golden, CLU, and others. In attendance are a number of other careerists, including young men like myself, who are striving for the higher levels of success achieved by these leaders. At the case clinics we are all given the opportunity to call in a "pinch hitter," these major league insurance salesmen, to demonstrate at bat the techniques which have sold millions.

Case One

Mr. A, a building contractor, was referred to me by a client who said that Mr. A was doing quite well and might well be in a position to own more life insurance. Mr. A was 53 years of age, married, with no children. He had an estate of $150,000 and kept it quite liquid. His insurance portfolio consisted of a total of $50,000 in paid-up or nearly paid-up policies. While reviewing his policies I had him take a medical examination to determine insurability as a foundation for later recommendations. In this way, I could qualify him for my ideas. As a matter of course, I ordered out a $10,000 whole life policy, feeling that this certainly was in line with what Mr. A could afford. He was approved standard, and when I offered the policy with my estate planning idea (that of using this additional insurance to pay for estate taxes), he flatly turned me down. Mr. A just wasn't interested!

This situation was presented at the case clinic. Karl Bach asked me for the file and said he would contact me after he had a chance to study the case further. My "pinch hitter" was at bat!

Three weeks later, at our general "free energy sales forum," the results of Karl's handling of this case were presented. Karl had placed a $50,000 policy with $2,400 of premium, paid annually.

This is how he did it: Mr. A did not believe in life insurance as such. He was savings conscious and liked the feeling of having a lot of liquid funds, money on which he could put his hands. Karl catered to Mr. A's *wants*. A program was built around a 20-pay life plan with double premiums payable annually for ten years. Mr. A would pay two premiums annually, with all premiums after the first discounted at the company's high 5 per cent per annum compound discount rate.

By this approach, an "auxiliary cash fund" was created and satisfied Mr. A's desire for cash liquidity. In ten years the policy would be fully paid, and nineteen of the twenty premiums would have been discounted to a constantly increasing extent. Of course, if the insured should die, the extra added attraction is $50,000 payable immediately to his wife.

The amount paid each year is calculated to be the exact amount needed to pay two additional annual premiums and complete all premium deposits at the end of 10 years.

115

The results of this case, incidentally, earned me $1,500 of bonus commissions, thanks to my pinch hitter. I might add that it also taught me a valuable lesson. My pinch hitter did not get paid out of my earnings. I got paid from his!

Case Two

Mr. B, age 64, a grandfather, wanted to do something for his five grand-children. He wanted to provide a college educational fund for each grandchild and give them a start on which to build a strong financial structure. I suggested he buy a policy on his life and name the grandchildren as owners and beneficiaries. If grandpa died, the grandchildren would be assured of his goals for them. Mr. B wanted something guaranteed and therefore was against mutual funds, etc. He was examined and qualified for our preferred underwriting, infrequent indeed at age 64. Upon receipt of the policy, I dashed down to deliver this "natural close." Mr. B took the policy and gave me his check. Late that evening, I got a phone call from him at my home. He said he had discussed the idea with his wife and that she was dead set against his signing his "death certificate." He said that his grandchildren would be amply taken care of by his will and that he did not want to "sign his life away" to them while he was still alive and kicking. He asked me to return his check.

The next week, I presented the case at the clinic. Ed Golden, our moderator, a life and qualifying member of the MDRT and CLU with over 30 years experience in the life insurance field, went to bat for me. He called Mr. B. during our meeting, using one of those telephone amplifying devices, in order that we would all hear exactly what was said. He suggested that Mr. B create an "Individually-owned-guaranteed-educational-fund" for each of the grandchildren. Grandpa would contribute to the fund annually. Each grandchild would have an immediate $25,000 estate which would start building cash values for his or her education right away. If grandpa died, he was to have a codicil in his will instructing his executor to continue the program or pay up the policies. Mr. B liked this idea, as it solved the problem facing him. He would no longer "sign away his life" for the benefit of his grandchildren. This case resulted in $125,000 of production with over $2,500 in premiums.

By the age of 27, I had completed 8 years in the life insurance business. During these formative years, I have made an effort to expose myself to every situation that can be found in the professional life insurance sales career. This idea of using the case clinic or "team" method of closing difficult sales has certainly proven one of the most unique and profitable I have experienced. My advice to any young life insurance salesman is never be so proud that you can't call in a "pinch hitter." The winning run in many a baseball game has come from just such a source. Cooperative effort will evolve new sales strategies and result in better education, increased status, dignity, and earning capacity.

This is how John Todd, one of the life insurance profession's all-time greats, introduces the expert!

"Bill, you know I am in the life insurance business and I suppose that like most anyone else you have so many friends in my business that you know you'd go broke if you tried to buy from them all. I have not called on you before, because I certainly don't want to add to that problem for you—and you know I have not been in this business long enough to be sure that I could do a good job for you as I would want to do for anyone that I consider to be such a good friend.

"But I have an associate in my company who is just terrific. He has the most remarkable ability to help smart men like you in solving their financial problems that I have ever seen.

"I have no idea if you are in the market for additional life insurance right now, but I don't care, because I know that you still have a great future ahead of you—and if you have, it's a cinch that someday you'll want to own more insurance than you can afford right now. Isn't that so?

"What I would like to do is to get you together with Mr. Jones. He can do more to help inform you on ways and means to improve your chances for financial success than anyone I know. Either you'll find that your present plan is the perfect one for you, or that it can be improved. In either case, you'll be better off, won't you?

"There's no cost to you, of course, for gaining from this kind of experience. All he asks is that if at some future time, as a result of his ideas, you decide added life insurance will solve your problems, other things being equal, we would get the business. That's fair enough, isn't it?

"How about lunch together next Wednesday, or would it be better if we came to your office on Thursday morning?"

(Everybody can make more sales and can avoid losing them . . . while learning from the pro's. Using an expert or calling in a pinch-hitter can help your growth in the life insurance business tremendously. It has "made" me.)

Robert B. Williams, CLU, and life member of the Million Dollar Round Table in Menlo Park, called me one day and presented the following situation. We call it the case of Mr. R.H.

Bob said: "I have a prospect here, Karl, whose company, the Modern Electronics Company, is considering buying some life insurance on him. I have the feeling that I cannot succeed in this situation, but I believe you can."

I asked Bob why he felt I could place the business. He said: "A general insurance broker with whom I have been working mentioned the fact that several other life insurance men had called on this firm to place a large key man policy but they had not succeeded. This general insurance man knows there is a real need for the life insurance and that the man who can sell it will be well-rewarded."

Bob gave me all the information on the prospect and I went to work at once. One of the first things that one should do with every new prospect is to make the call without delay. I was told that all business decisions in the firm were made by the business manager, a young Harvard Business School graduate, named Hal Brown, whose reputation for expertise in the company was significant.

I immediately decided on my course of action. I always keep in mind and often read my "Ten Thoughts before Making a Call." I have them before me on the desk at all times. I need to remind myself because it is human to forget. Regardless of what we think, there is no one who always follows a natural procedure.

I called the firm, a medium-sized electronics manufacturer situated not far from my home on the San Francisco Peninsula, and asked for Hal Brown. I introduced myself and the following dialogue developed.

"Mr. Brown, my name is Karl Bach. I am a buyer of life insurance, and I have reason to believe that your firm is contemplating the purchase of key man life insurance on your president and that you are the man in charge of making the decision. Isn't that correct?"

I waited for Hal Brown to do the talking. Yes, he was the man, but, as so often happens, he tried to put me off.

"Mr. Brown, I was told you are a graduate of the Harvard Business School. Isn't that correct?

He immediately confirmed that this was the case and told me how great a school it is and he took a considerable amount of time to tell me all about the Harvard Business School. I then knew that I had hit a hot button. I could not help pointing out with pride that my oldest son had graduated cum laude from Harvard. This little incident established a slight bond of friendship between us over the telephone. You could feel the warmth over the wires.

I continued: "Hal, since you are a very busy man, I presume you have no intention of wasting a lot of time with many insurance salesmen."

He agreed.

"As a buyer of life insurance, I have a suggestion for you. Undoubtedly, you have many proposals regarding the insurance on your company's president. Here is what I would like you to do. I would like to have the opportunity to present to you a proposal signed by the president of the insurance company from which I will try to purchase the best insurance plan for your firm and present it to you without any obligation. You will be the sole judge. My proposal will differ from any others that you have seen. It will have a number that, should you decide to purchase, will immediately obligate the insurance company for the amount of insurance your firm has to have. Let me ask you this, Hal. What is the maximum amount of insurance that the firm is considering?"

He said, "We are considering a million dollars."

I continued, "Hal, it certainly would be a feather in your cap to choose a buyer of life insurance who has had real experience in cases of this size."

He agreed that it would.

I said, "Now, let me tell you how I operate. I would like to have Mr. R.H., your president, come to San Francisco next Wednesday or Friday, whichever time is convenient, and I will set up an appointment with my special medical examiner who will give him all the necessary tests. This will determine what his exact rate will be. After this has been accomplished, it will be anywhere from three to four weeks before I will have a policy number for you that will obligate the insurance company for one million dollars. I will then call you for an appointment and at that time it will be up to your good business judgment to decide if you want to transfer the risk from your firm to the insurance company."

After a short dialogue as to why the medical examinations were necessary, he agreed to set up the required appointment.

I met Mr. R.H. at the doctor's office in order to get acquainted with him. I wanted to make certain that a proper rapport would be established between him and the doctor. There are so many unexpected hurdles that we salesmen have to overcome. So many little unforeseen events can kill the sale. An unfriendly nurse, a retail credit report, and many other

119

unexpected events have killed many a sure fire sale. The examination was successful in this case. And so were all the other required tests. This case was placed at the first interview. The premium was $28,000.

For the delivery interview, I brought Bob Williams with me. I wanted him to get acquainted with the firm and the people since we were going to share this commission and all future commissions on business written on this firm. I had a hunch that there would be other key people to be insured as well as personal insurance on the employees of the firm.

Bob Williams will gladly tell you that in no other year of his long and successful life insurance career had he been as financially successful as he was on this case. For me, the rewards were not financial alone.

They were threefold. I had had the pleasure of helping a colleague; I had been able to provide the necessary capital for the client in the form of life insurance; and I had the pleasure of making new friends.

When a prospect asks you questions you are not equipped to answer, your best solution is to say, "I don't know, but I know someone who does."

You can bluff, of course, but bluffing is poor fuel for the fires of free energy salesmanship. Even if it is necessary to share the credit or commissions with the man you call in, half of something is always better than all of nothing. And nothing is what bluffing usually will get you. I find that there is communication in an interview other than the spoken word. The fact that you are bluffing will transmit itself.

To prevent losing the sale, there are two important things to remember. The first is to call in another salesman or expert when, if not before, things begin to go wrong and not wait until the whole house is burning down. The second is to know how to support him and build him up.

This is an age of specialization. Few of us—even the most skilled do-it-yourselfers—can do all the work by ourselves. You and the expert will accomplish many otherwise impossible sales. And remember, some day you too will be an expert extending assistance to others.

TEN THOUGHTS BEFORE THE INTERVIEW FOR
BETTER RESULTS IN SELLING

1. Think. What is my objective? I will follow through.

2. Think. Is my timing right? I must have a plan of action.

3. Think. Can I delegate any responsibilities? Is such delegation in the best interest of time and money? Shall I call in an expert?

4. Think. Is there a better way? Have I explored all possible avenues?

5. Think. Do I know enough about my prospect, his needs, his business and his interests? If I Don't, who does?

6. Think. To whom can I refer for proper prestige before seeing my client? A third party influence is invaluable.

7. Think. Have I done everything possible to qualify my prospect? Do I have some of the important information or all that is available?

8. Think. Have I planned to see him under the most favorable circumstances possible?

9. Think. Have I put myself in my prospect's place? Can I view my proposal from his point of view? Am I prepared to *listen?*

10. Think. Am I prepared to talk with enthusiasm, sincerity and humility? My responsibility is to solve a problem. The solution will create the sale.

49—Learning While You Are Teaching

My associate, Maurice Edelstein, a Life and Qualifying Member of the MDRT, has spent his entire selling career in my office. I hired him originally to do my detail work but I soon realized that Morrie, who was 23 years old at the time, had a knack for selling. That is what he has been doing ever since.

Morrie has a great deal of respect for the other person's time. During the many years we have worked together, the only time I had to spend with him was when he could not think a problem through by himself. Many salesmen who are more experienced than Morrie will frequently take the easy way out and take others' time rather than think a problem through by themselves. If they did, it would be much more rewarding for them and would do them more good in the long run.

When he calls in an associate or specialist, a man like Morrie has such conviction that he is so able to sell his associate to the prospect that a sale will be made with ease in most cases.

Morrie is unique in many ways. In my opinion, one of his great assets is his compassion for the other guy. I have never seen a man who has as many friends as Morrie and has so many people seeking his help. This generous amount of time that he has given others has taken away from his selling time, but it is giving him much greater satisfaction than merely making more money.

There is no man more successful than Morrie. Of course, we can measure success in various ways. I measure it by the personal satisfaction and happiness we derive from what we are doing.

Morrie's true power is in his dependability and that quality which makes him give his very best to every day regardless of how he feels. There is nothing that can deter him from fulfilling his daily task of helping others.

In working with Morrie and my other associates, I have learned a great deal. When they come to me with a sales problem, often I am able to view the situation with third party objectivity. From this perspective, the solution is obvious in many instances. But because I am an expert in their minds, I have to play that role and put my underworked brain into operation.

W. Donald Sparkman, one of my long time associates and Life and Qualifying Member of the Million Dollar Round Table, is probably one of the most independent life insurance men I know. Very seldom does he seek my advice because of his respect for my time and the value that he puts on his own. However, one day he ran into a prospect who baffled him. He knew that there was a lot of business to be written but he felt that his rapport with the prospect was not as good as it could be. He immediately decided the best thing for him to do was to sell me to the prospect.

As it happened, I had heard of this prospect in the past and had even met him on one or two occasions. Mr. Gallo was a very prominent businessman who, with his brother, ran a very successful manufacturing corporation in Oakland.

Don and I discussed the strategy of how best to make a client of Mr. Gallo, who in the last ten years had avoided the purchase of any life insurance. I told Don that the only way to get anywhere with him was to have him come to my office in San Francisco. If Don could make that sale, there was no question that we could make him a good client.

Don asked, "What shall I do if he does not want to come to San Francisco?" My answer was very simple. "This is what you have to sell. And I know that you can sell it. If we don't get him into our "ball park," we are going to be no different than all the other salesmen who have tried and failed to sell him; we will never get the sale."

Don had a tough time convincing Mr. Gallo to come across the Bay to San Francisco, but knowing that this was the only way to get the sale, he succeeded in getting him to my office, where we completed the first sale we had made together in quite a while. Mr. Gallo and his brother both became clients of ours; over the years we have added many other clients through their recommendations.

The point in this case is that frequently a simple decision such as where to play the game can make the difference between winning and losing. By being different from the other salesmen, we seemed to offer our prospect something more valuable. Through Don's early observation that his prestige with the client was not effective enough, he was able to stay in the ball game and eventually win by bringing in a pinch-hitter.

In many other instances where agents have asked me to work with them, I have insisted upon my colleague making the appointment with his prospect in my office. I am quite sure that this simple procedure has been instrumental in making for an almost 100% closing ratio in situations of that type. The important factor is that by selling me to the prospect and bringing the prospect into my office, my colleague has established a flow of free energy that invariably leads to a sale.

50—An Example Of Salesmanship That Has Been With Me Throughout My Life Insurance Career

While I was still selling Fuller Brushes, I became friendly with a longtime life insurance agent of one of the major companies. My friendship with this man extended over several years until he died. I had purchased a policy from another agent prior to meeting this gentleman and my only connections were occasional telephone calls. When I got married, he bought me a most beautiful gift. However, the other agent, who was none other than my future tutor, Jerome Breyer, did not even send me a card. About two weeks after my marriage, my friend called me asking to see me concerning a life insurance purchase. I had no intention of buying life insurance. I had just spent all my money furnishing an apartment and told him to delay his visit until sometime in the future.

The following evening, Jerome Breyer called. "Karl," he said, "you're home?"

I said, "Yes."

He said, "I'll be over in five minutes."

He hung up. Five minutes later he walked in the door, congratulated my wife for having made such a fine choice and, after a few informalities, created in me a desire to save more money by means of life insurance. Then he told me that even if I desired to buy at the present time, I could not do so unless I qualified after a very rigid medical examination. The doctor would be seeing me the following morning.

That is how I purchased my second life insurance policy. I never gave the friend who had sent me such a beautiful wedding gift the opportunity to present his wares. Jerome sold me the idea of saving and he made it very simple by seeing me on the spot. More than that, he sold me the idea later of going into the insurance business, for which I will be forever indebted to him. This purchase has been the best investment I probably will ever make because it has taught me a very valuable lesson in selling which I have repeated and repeated successfully. I have always followed the saying, "What someone else can do, I can do."

51—Respect The Expert In Other Fields But Stick To Selling!

One of my bigger cases not long ago resulted from tending to selling and trying to avoid technicalities. I had an appointment across the Bay with the president of a large industrial concern and when I arrived, I was informed that my prospect had been called away unexpectedly. Here I was, twenty miles from my office. This could have been a waste of time but I decided to make this call count anyway.

On the other side of the street was another large industrial concern. I inquired as to the identity of the president of this firm and was given his name. I walked across the street and handed the receptionist my card. I asked her if she would please tell Mr. X that Mr. Bach was here to see him.

Much to my surprise the receptionist came back and ushered me into the president's office. He was a man of about 50 years of age. He seemed to possess much charm and personality. I could not help liking him at once. There is no question that the fact he had received me so nicely added to this feeling. Mr. X opened the conversation:

"Our company is contemplating some insurance on my life. I am delighted to talk to a salesman. If you have a few minutes, Mr. Bach, I would like to have you read a proposal that was made for our company by a CLU and I would like to have your opinion."

He handed me a twenty page report, beautifully typed on an Executive typewriter and packaged in an attractive folder. I secretly thought how much I would like to be able to do something like that. However, I learned early in my career that selling requires the personal explanation of any proposal and a proposal, regardless of how well it is designed, cannot replace a salesman.

I glanced quickly through the pages. The particular sections that flew before me dealt with income tax laws. The entire proposal reminded me of a legal document and I had a very tough time indeed understanding thoroughly just what my competitor was trying to do. I decided to hand the proposal back to my prospect. I said:

"Mr. X, this is an outstanding job, one which would do credit to any of the better law firms specializing in taxation. However, I feel that at this point, your interest would be best served if we could establish at once what the exact rate would be for a million dollars worth of life insurance on you. Once we establish that point, we can determine, with your legal counsel, on what basis your life insurance should be owned and to whom it should be payable."

Mr. X fully agreed that making sure he could qualify medically for the life insurance was something that should be established first. I notified him immediately of the results of all the tests and then I received an okay from our underwriters for a million dollars. I ordered the contract payable to and owned by his corporation. If there were any changes to be made by the attorneys as to ownership and beneficiary designations, they could be made afterwards.

He went along 100% with everything I said. My competitor never entered the picture. Mr. X has become an excellent client of our office and I am enjoying additional benefits of this cold canvass call because Mr. X thinks a lot of me as a salesman and has recommended me to many of his substantial friends.

I do not think that I did anything for Mr. X that any other salesman could not have done but he wanted a salesman to take care of his life insurance, not a technician. He told me later that the fact that he did have competent tax counsel and legal advisors made him want an insurance man who would bring forth new ideas which would challenge and stimulate these advisors. I am convinced that more salesmen would do well to take advantage of this knowledge by making sure they stick to selling.

52—Free Energy From Third Party Influence

Since most prospects have been conditioned to mistrust salesmen, it is not easy to create confidence and give proof that a salesman knows his business and really has the interest of his prospect at heart. The use of third party influence at the proper time will often help to get the proper results.

When selling a medical examination there are all kinds of interesting objections. Often, a prospect will state that he has just had an examination and that he is in perfect health and, therefore, there is no reason to take another medical examination. In this type of situation, it is best not to disagree with the prospect and to bring forth strong, motivating evidence that will sell the medical examination.

One very powerful motivating weapon is a letter from our underwriting department stating that a prospect has been declined. I always make sure that the name on such a letter is covered up to protect the privacy of the client. I read the contents of the letter to the prospect and make a statement such as: "Do you know, Mr. Prospect, that the gentleman who was declined life insurance is a prominent businessman in the city. He told me exactly the same thing you are telling me now. Unfortunately, I went along with him and did everything his way. He had decided to buy a $200,000 policy and he even qualified on his medical examinations. But there was one little line on his EKG which proved him to be uninsurable."

When I still feel resistance, I come up with another case to further hammer home my point. I always use current cases. I just had one for the books. A prominent physician who thought himself a perfect risk was found to be a diabetic. The insurance examination revealed the condition to him for the first time.

53—You've Got To Be Lucky
(But The More Calls You Make, The Luckier You'll Get)

My associate, Morrie Edelstein, came to my office the other day to tell me he had run into one of my clients, the controller of the JCY Company. He mentioned to Maurie that his company had just acquired a company in Los Angeles and that they needed a million dollars on the president of the corporation. Unfortunately, the controller hadn't thought of me but mentioned their need to their general insurance broker. However, he told Maurie that he would see if we couldn't get this business anyway.

127

Rather than waiting to hear from my client, I immediately went to the telephone and offered my services to him. He was very apologetic for not having thought of me right away but said if I could call him the following Monday, he would have had a chance to talk to the top management; he would see to it that I would be able to compete with their general insurance broker. I inquired as to the name of the prospective insured and his company, which he gladly gave to me.

The following day I was in Los Angeles at a party which was attended by perhaps one hundred people. There was a strangely dressed man talking to a beautiful young lady. He had long hair and looked like an artist to me. Later on I was introduced to the young lady and asked her who the gentleman that she had been talking with was. She replied that his name was Arthur Langdon; he was president of the JCY Company. At first nothing registered in my mind but about ten minutes later it suddenly dawned on me that that was the name my controller friend had mentioned. Could this be the same man? The name was the same; the company was the same. Yes, this must be the man. I asked the young lady to introduce me and, sure enough, here was my prospect.

I told him about the conversation that had taken place in San Francisco; it flattered him that his company's new owners thought enough of him to want to insure him for $1,000,000. I made an appointment for the following morning because I felt that I might just as well take care of the details of the medical examination before my competitor beat me to the punch.

We got along beautifully at our appointment. I pointed out to Mr. Langdon that the sale of his business had fixed a definite market price for it and, consequently, created the immediate need for a sizeable life insurance policy on Mrs. Langdon to cover the estate and inheritance tax liabilities that go with a large estate.

The result of this accidental meeting—where luck and opportunity met—was very gratifying. It also proves again that for a salesman, exposure to people is the only way to show one's wares. A salesman with the greatest know-how who does not have the opportunity to practice that know-how with his prospects will never know how good he is. And all his know-how will be wasted.

PART VI

Selling While Listening To Your Own Questions

54—Developing Free Energy And Making It Work

To help a prospect buy, you must help him by creating in him the desire to discover the problem which only life insurance can solve. You must help him by developing the problem slowly. Then suddenly he will see it clearly. The following are examples of the kinds of questions to which the prospect will react favorably. These may be used before beginning on a sales track.

"Mr. Prospect, here is an idea I would like your opinion on:

Would you be willing to share an idea with me?

(Then give the idea and ask:)

How do you see this idea working for you?

How do you see this idea in your scheme of things?

(After you have listened carefully to his answers, you say:)

Would you give me your idea of what we just covered?"

Naturally, after each question, let the prospect do a lot of talking and make mental and *written* notes while listening very attentively.

You must also help the prospect understand what he has discovered. He has to have a clear picture in order to act in the right way. *It has to become his own idea.*

If the prospect has a question, don't let him get you off the track. Postpone answering his question with a question. You might say, "Mr. Prospect, if you don't mind, before I answer that, I want to make sure I understand what you mean. Is this what you mean? Why do you feel the way you do? Is there any doubt in your mind about this? To be sure there is no doubt in your mind about it, tell me." And please listen to the prospect.

Or better yet, you might say, "Mr. Prospect, would you please make a note of your question so I won't forget to answer it and I will come back to it later." In many instances the prospect will forget about the question entirely or it will have been answered. Your objective has to be to make him see that life insurance is the best and only solution to a problem.

Since life insurance is really a monopoly and no other property or commodity can do what life insurance does, there is no substitute for life insurance. When you get to the close, you have to use all your closing techniques. I have found that making something hard to get and challenging your prospect with the idea that he might not qualify is often the best closing device.

55—Questions, Questions, Questions—Drawing Free Energy From Your Prospects

It took me many years to learn that the use of questions can be of tremendous value in salesmanship. I consider that this discovery, and using it continually, has been responsible to the greatest extent for my success in selling. I will never forget that my first introduction to life insurance selling included a sales talk which I was supposed to memorize and give to as many people as possible.

I could not help noticing, within a very short period of time, that very seldom was I able to give this sales talk completely; for some reason or other, the prospect always got me off the track, or I could feel that there was no need to complete the entire length of the sales talk to make the sale. I noticed, in many situations where I gave the talk, that the client was not only not interested, but he paid absolutely no attention and was bored with what I had to say. And when I did not make the sale and the client more or less urged me to leave, I often wondered what I had done wrong. I gradually came to the conclusion that if there was a way to find out what the prospect was thinking, what was going on in his mind, what he was interested in, what his feelings were about his family, what his financial objectives were, I would be able to shortcut any sales talk and not fall into the trap that most salesmen fall into when they do not make the sale. The client is selling them; they are not selling the client.

To open an interview, I have found several questions that cut right down to the meat of things.

"Mr. Prospect, do you now own some life insurance? What was your primary reason for buying it?"

Then I shut up and let the prospect tell me what his reasons were for buying his existing insurance. Keeping your mouth shut long enough to hear him talk is very, very important because he will tell you what motivated him and probably will give you a reason he can be motivated now.

The next question is: "If you were to buy some more life insurance, why would you buy it?"

Again, his answers will give you the clue as to the direction your sales talk should follow. If I get a negative answer, then I ask:

"Mr. Prospect, since you are not buying any more at this time, if you were to buy again in the future, why would you buy?"

And again I am an excellent listener, because he will tell me what I could never find out otherwise.

Some additional questions that are also useful in the opening inverview are: "Mr. Prospect, what are your feelings regarding life insurance? Are you satisfied with your present life insurance program? Are you satisfied with the amount of insurance you now own? What are your objectives regarding your financial future, for yourself and for your family?"

Another opening of this type is, "Mr. Prospect, I assume that you now own some life insurance. Is this correct? I imagine you do not mind talking about it, do you?" If the answer is, yes, he does mind, your reply should just be "why?"

I am quite sure that nearly every salesman has a pet set of questions. If not, he should develop a set he can use continually. The more often he uses these questions and the longer he conditions himself to listening to the answers, the easier his sales efforts will become. Resistance in the sales process will melt away so that it becomes one that needs very little high pressure. The pressure will not come from you. It will be created by the prospect, in himself, and will act for his benefit in helping you to get better results.

I recommend here that everyone in selling break down long sentences into their component simple questions. Here is an example of what I mean.

Let us assume that I am trying to sell the virtues of life insurance and I use the following phrase:

"Mr. Prospect, life insurance is the only medium whereby a man can save money each year and should he die prematurely, his family will receive the full amount that he had set out to save had he lived."

This statement broken down into simple questions would look as follows:

"Mr. Prospect, what is the difference between life insurance and a normal savings medium? Have you ever heard of an investment medium that matures at full face value at death regardless of the amount of money that has been paid into it?"

These are the same thoughts, except that by changing them into question form, the prospect has to participate and becomes a partner throughout the sales interview.

In many instances when we are using questions to begin the interview and during the interview, we might preface the question with words such as, "Mr. Prospect, I am quite sure that you are aware that you can provide 100% dollars by depositing only 1%," or, "Mr. Prospect, did you know that your estate can be arranged in such a manner that it will escape the tax collector completely?" and so on.

"Mr. Prospect, what methods are you using to accumulate capital?" "Mr. Prospect, what do you think might be wrong with your present methods of saving?" "Are you taking advantage of recent tax laws regarding capital accumulation?" "Have you explored the modern way of accumulating capital?"

56—Free Energy—How To Get It Flowing

Here is a selection of questions that I have been using successfully in getting the prospect to become a buyer of life insurance—questions that can be used in the approach, during the interview and in the close. I know that if you adopt them, they can work miracles for you. However, it is of utmost importance that after each question is asked you keep your mouth shut long enough that your prospect is able to do a lot of talking and you do a lot of listening. Only then will you tap his reservoir of energy. And only then can you direct this energy to help you close the sale. When you close the sale, you are helping your client, his family and his business.

It has been said that a salesman should have an assistant with four inch adhesive tape, after a question is asked, the assistant should tape his mouth so that he has to keep it shut.

Series Of Important Questions:

Questions to ask to get an interview or make an appointment.

Questions to ask during an interview.

Questions to ask to sell a medical examination or use in closing a sale.

The Three Most Important Questions To Open A Sales Interview:

"Mr. Prospect, you now own some life insurance; what was your primary reason for buying it?"

"If you were to buy some more insurance, why would you buy it?" (If the answer is in the negative, then ask:)

"Since you are not buying any more insurance at this time, if you were to buy again in the future sometime, why would you buy it?"

Important Questions To Create Interest And Disturb:

"Do you have an open mind?"

"Has anyone approached you in the last few years and offered to help you buy additional life insurance?"

"Mr. Prospect, I assume that you own some life insurance." Reply—"Correct." "I imagine you do not mind talking about it, do you?" If the answer you receive is ... "Yes, I do mind," then your answer is just, "Why?"

"Mr. Prospect, if you have a problem you want to solve it. If you don't have one you will want to know that, too. That's why it will pay you to talk to me."

"Mr. Prospect, I'd like to have your opinion of a plan my company is offering. I'm not going to try to 'sell' you anything because you impress me as the kind of man who makes his own judgments and arrives at his own conclusions. However, your opinion would be very helpful to me in my sales work. May I show you the details and ask for your suggestions? It will take only a few minutes."

"I have a new idea about which I wish to give you a few highlights."

"When did you last purchase life insurance? What was your primary reason for buying it?"

"Have you ever heard of a fishing or golfing policy?"

"You wouldn't deny me the opportunity of becoming acquainted with you, would you, Mr. Prospect?"

"Mr. Prospect, what are your views on life insurance property?"

"Mr. Prospect, I am here today to buy your lifetime earnings. What would you take for them? Could we negotiate?"

When you call on a businessman, say, "How long would you continue the salary of Mr. Employee if he were to be disabled for a long period of time?"

"Would you like to create a rich man's estate today?"

"Mr. Prospect, do you own life insurance? Tell me why you own it."

"Did you know I sell instant estates?"

"How would you like to make your life insurance pay out not only to your wife if you die, but to you if she dies?"

"Mr. Prospect, isn't it true that your company has regular accountants who work the year around? And isn't it true also that once each year you have a qualified firm of accountants audit and go through your books to make certain that the work of your own accountants throughout the year has been done correctly? Well, Mr. Prospect, I want to go over and audit the work that your insurance advisor has done for you to make certain that he hasn't forgotten something vital to your program.

136

"Would you object to owning more life insurance if you didn't have to pay for more?"

"Mr. Prospect, how much of your estate assets will be free from creditors' claims?"

"Mr. Prospect, would you object if we improved the quality of your present insurance program?"

"Is your life insurance as modern as the plumbing in your house?"

"Would you like to have a tax scholarship for your grandchildren (short term trust) granted free by Uncle Sam?"

"Have you ever heard of the ice cube way of transferring capital?"

"Do you have key woman life insurance?"

"Would you pay ten cents for a dollar?"

"How many times earnings are you selling for?"

"What percentage of your total income would you like to have continued permanently for your own benefit later on in life?"

"Do you know if you are buying your present insurance with taxed dollars or tax-free dollars?"

"Do you know if your policies are sanforized?"

"Would you object to owning an extra $100,000 worth of life insurance?"

"If you have life insurance now, I have an idea whereby you can complete all payments in approximately eleven years instead of paying for life by just doubling the premium."

"How old is your youngest policy?"

"If someone would agree to mail a one dollar bill to you each month at age 65, would you be willing to pay the postage on it in advance?"

"When you fly, do you take out travel insurance on each trip? How much do you take out and why? Would you like to have it at lower rates forever?"

"Are you saving any money other than in life insurance?"

"Do you know what your last number is?" "--706"

"Do you have the three free extras in your life insurance policy?"

"What kind of double indemnity do you have? The regular kind or the all-purpose kind? Do you know the difference?"

"Mr. Prospect, will your family receive 100% of the money from your policies or will your family share them with 200,000,000 strangers?"

"Mr. Prospect, will your family receive 100% of the money from your policies or will Uncle Sam take 30% and leave your family with only 70%?"

"When you came into this building or when you go into any large building, do you walk the stairs or do you take the elevator?"

"Airlines insure passengers for $75,000 while in flight. Would you like a plan that would cover you while you fly, after landing, after leaving the aircraft and on the freeway—24 hours a day—for a much lower cost?"

"Mr. Prospect, how much money are you now spending for life insurance?" (let him talk)

"What kind of policies do you now have? Twenty-pay life, ordinary life, etc?"

"Mr. Prospect, if I came to you with a fabulous business idea, could you come up with $10,000 in cash within ten hours on the conditions that you get it from your own resources and that you not mortgage your home? If you can do it, I will explain to you the most marvelous business idea you have ever heard. If

138

you cannot raise the cash, then I won't explain. Could you do it?"
If the answer is "No," then ask the prospect, "Why not?" Then
you proceed to sell him opportunity money.

"Mr. Prospect, here is an idea that I would like to have your
opinion on."

"Have you ever seen how life insurance works?"

"Have you ever seen an X-ray of a life insurance policy?"

"How would you like to magnify the purchasing power of the
life insurance you now own—through proper planning?

"Mr. Prospect, what do you want life insurance to accomplish
for you?" (let him talk) "What is your primary objective?"

"Mr. Prospect, will your creditors have first call on your policy
proceeds or will your wife get the money?"

"Does your insurance go directly to your family or does it go
through the courts?"

"Do I have to assume that you are afraid to discuss your life
insurance with me?"

"Would you mind giving me the time to ask you just two
questions? What is there that everybody will always need . . .
whether male or female, young or old, fat or thin, short or tall,
rich or poor?" INCOME! "Why will they always need income?"

"Mr. Prospect, if someone would agree to mail you a $1 bill
each month after you are 65, would you be willing to pay the
postage on it in advance? If I were selling bundles of $100 bills
for 3 cents on the dollar, how many would you want?"

"Did Mr. X (name a big competitor of Mr. Prospect) mention
me to you?"

"What have you done about the mortgage on your property you
didn't sign? Have you considered the latest innovations in life
insurance?"

"Was your last life insurance purchase before 1960?"

"What do you think of life insurance? What do you like about life insurance? What do you hate about life insurance?"

"Mr. Prospect, what are your feelings regarding life insurance? Are you satisfied with your present life insurance program? Are you satisfied with the amount of insurance you now own?"

"What are your objectives in creating a sound financial future for yourself and your family?"

"If I had a plan that would help you establish such an objective, and you could save $50 to $100 a month, would you have an open mind to considering what it can do for you?"

"What do you think of life insurance?"

"Why do you own life insurance?"

"Why would you like to own more life insurance?"

"Why did you buy your last policy? What appealed to you about it?"

"Why would you want to buy in the future?"

"When will you buy?"

"Why will you buy it then?"

"What would you like to accomplish?"

"What is your objective?"

Free Energy Statements:

"Here is what I suggest . . ."

"This is what I recommend . . ."

"This is my personal recommendation . . ."

57—Free Energy—How To Keep It Flowing

"Has this ever occurred to you?"

"Have you ever thought of this?"

"Have you ever looked at it in this light?"

"Did you ever think of this?"

"Mr. Prospect, is there any reason why we cannot do business if you decide to use the ideas and plans that I have developed for you?"

"Mr. Prospect, may I ask you to forget completely for a few minutes that there is such a thing as life insurance."

"How long does your family need income? As long as you live, or as long as your family lives?"

"Does your key man life insurance equal *your* life insurance?"

"How would you like to work for the next ten years of your life without pay?"

"Are you immunized against stock deterioration?"

"Wouldn't it be nice to have somebody pay your bills for you?"

"What worries you the most?"

"How long would your family receive your salary if you were called away from your business by an accident or heart attack?"

"Have you measured your present life insurance against the job it must do?"

"If you sold me the rights to all your future paychecks, what price would you set? Have you arranged for your wife to get these rights in case of your premature death?"

"Did you know that you are head of one of the greatest corporations in the world, an American family? Your wife is treasurer and your children are the stockholders. What have you done to protect the assets of this corporation?"

"Are you working for money, or is money working for you?"

"Can you tell me the day you are going to die?"

"I imagine, Mr. Prospect, that you have definite plans for building up capital. Perhaps real estate or mutual funds. Am I right?"

"How would you like to own your own finance company?"

"Mr. Prospect, what percentage of your total income will continue without your working power?"

"Do you know how to use your life insurance to earn tax-free interest equivalent to a 5% tax-free municipal or state bond?"

"Would you be surprised if I told you that you probably have $25,000 to $30,000 more life insurance protection for your wife and family than you realize?"

"Would you like to be rich, or would you like to be richer?"

"Do you know that man has two lives—a physical one and a financial one? Do you know what the difference is between the two?"

"Do you know that thousands of people pool thousands of dollars to share thousands of risks and then they call it insurance?"

"Do you know that the person who doesn't buy life insurance puts up thousands of dollars to cover just one risk?"

"Do you ever borrow money? Did you know that finance companies can charge up to 24%?"

"Do you do any investing now?"

"What do you hope to realize on your investments?"

"When was the last time you looked at your business agreement?"

"When was the last time you looked at your will? Let's get it out and see if it is up to date."

"What is the current rate of interest at your bank?"

"I presume that you have made a will, Mr. Prospect." When the answer is, "Yes," as it is likely to be, then say: "Well, I think we had better get it out and have a look at it to see whether or not it needs refunding. After all, no matter what you hope your estate will accomplish through your will, the document isn't worth much if the funds aren't there to carry it out."

"Mr. Prospect, you wouldn't object if I could help you, would you?"

"Is this a sound plan in your judgment? Would this program be good for an executive (or a professional man) in your position?"

"When are you going to make the last payment on an install-ment purchase?"

"Do you have any objection to me personally?"

"Mr. Prospect, has it ever occurred to you that buying life insurance is applying for a paid-up credit card in the future?"

"Do you know what part of your estate is not yours tomorrow?"

"Did you know that it will cost you $_____ to hang on to what you now have?"

"May I suppose that you are using trusts to save taxes?"

"May I suppose that you have taken all steps to regain that part of your estate you are about to lose?"

"Have you considered the latest innovations in life insurance?"

143

"You own all the life insurance you need, but who will get it some day?"

"Don't you agree that if you are not going to die before your retirement, then it must be true that you will need income for your retirement?"

"What is your opinion? Can a wife that never has been widowed be as qualified to evaluate life insurance as a widow?"

"Would you buy an elephant worth $10,000? Probably not. Would you buy the same elephant for $2,000 if you could donate it to a zoo and get a tax deduction for $8,000 and your $2,000 back?"

"Have you ever been a trustee for somebody?"

"Have you ever heard of a product that removes speculation?"

"I don't believe in life insurance": "You are a businessman, Mr. Prospect. Instead of a belief, let us consider it from a business standpoint. Don't you think that makes sense?"

"I don't care to leave anything to my children":

"Do you operate your business on how little you can make or how much you can make? Why arrange your affairs on how little you can earn or on how little you can leave?"

"Do you take advantage of discounts while you are alive? Why force your family to refuse the discounts you could take the moment you close your eyes?"

"Is it better business to use your own 100 cents dollars or the 3 cents dollars that I might be able to deliver?"

"What key man in your organization is worth insuring? Is he a key man if he is not worth insuring?"

"Do you know if you are going to outlive your partner?"

"Do you know if your partner is going to outlive you?"

"Don't you agree that if you are not going to die before your partner, then it must be true that he is going to die before you?"

"If a man dies, is the loss partial or total? What are the chances of death?"

"Do you agree that you will either be: (1) a dead man; or, (2) an old man?"

"If you were a trustee of a large fund belonging to a widow and her children consisting of income producing real estate, would you carry fire insurance on such property? What would the judge of a probate court say if you didn't? What are the chances of a fire? (Maybe one in 100,000). What type of loss is there in case of a fire? (Property). How many fire losses are total? (One in a million). Don't you agree that most fire losses are partial losses and not total? Has it ever occurred to you that you are paying full premiums for mostly partial losses when you insured your real estate?"

USE SILENCE! ! !

58—Questions To Sell A Medical Or Use In Closing A Sale

"Is there any reason for you to believe you could not qualify medically?"

"Are you the kind of man who likes to take risks? Or are you the kind of man who doesn't like to work?"

"What do you fear the most?"

"Do you fear poverty more than disability?"

"Do you fear criticism more than old age?"

"Do you fear death more than old age?"

You might want to use this particular statement: "A man recently said, '(such and such . . .)'. What do you think of it, Mr. Prospect?"

"What in your imagination would be the worst thing that could ever happen to you during your lifetime? For a moment, your prospect probably will stop to think. However, before he gives you the answer, you give him the answer . . . like this: "Well, Mr. Prospect, let me just pose a situation and see if this might not qualify as the worst thing that could happen to you. If your wife should die and on that same day you should lose your job, don't you feel that would probably be the worst thing that could ever happen to you? Well, Mr. Prospect, this is what happens to your wife when you die. Now that's something to think about."

"Should a man be more considerate of his wife than of his widow, the mother of his children?"

"Had you lost a friend or relative in the last two years through death, would you have known how much life insurance he had? Had you known he had no insurance, would you have been willing to lend him the premium on a $100,000 policy had you known he was dying?"

"When the prospect says he wants to think it over, ask this question: "If you decide not to buy after thinking it over. What will your probable reason be for that decision?"

"Would you like for me to take your family's problem with me rather than leaving you to carry it alone?"

"Have you ever thought that by not buying you are putting yourself in the insurance business? Wouldn't it be better to let the specialists take care of what they know best?"

"First, forgetting all other considerations, do you feel that this is the *right* thing for you to do?" He invariably answers, "Yes," if I have not misjudged the situation. I then say, "There is just one more question, Mr. Prospect. Have you ever been sorry for doing the *right* thing?"

"Mr. Prospect, is there any reason why you would not do business with me?"

"Mr. Prospect, do you know of any other plan which will enable you to will $100,000 to your family before you earn it?"

"Would you sell any of your stocks or real estate now to pay a bill if you were short on cash? What would you do?"

"There are two kinds of widows: widows with homes and homeless widows. Which will your wife be?"

"Do you agree that it would be worth plenty to you to be able to stop worrying and have somebody worry for you?"

"Do you know any other way that you can will your family thousands of dollars before you earn them?"

"Did you ever hear of anyone worrying about the safety of his life insurance? You would *give* your life for your children; why not insure it for them?"

"How big an estate are you building? When do you think you will reach your objective? Have you considered the effects of income taxes? Have you considered the latest innovations in life insurance?"

"Why not cancel your life insurance and save the premiums?"

"Is the love for your family worth the loss of *only* the present enjoyment of a small part of your income?"

"Would you sell a piece of your real estate or some of your stocks for half their value *now* to pay a debt tomorrow you didn't have today?"

"Just three questions, Mr. Prospect:

1. Do you think you can pass an insurance medical exam?

2. Would you like to have tax-free dollars?

3. Do you like strangers better than your own family?"

147

"Do you agree that the man who does not risk anything, in reality, risks everything? In other words, the man who does not wish to risk anything will risk a lot more."

"Do you agree that the man who doesn't buy insurance puts himself in the insurance business? Do you agree that the premium he thinks he saves will come due all at one time? Do you agree that he is like an insurance company that carries no reserves and goes broke when the first big claim occurs?"

"Do you have more than THREE REASONS to think it over?"

"Do you know what the three reasons usually are?

1. Don't understand.

2. No money.

3. Don't want to buy from me.

"Do you know of any other reason?"

"Since you are not interested at this time, if you ever were interested again, why and for what reason would you buy life insurance?"

PART VII

Bach's Selling Variations

59—Come Along With Me On A Few Calls

It is Monday morning. I have had part of my breakfast at home and now I have to leave my comfortable house to start my selling day. I know that the product I am selling—life insurance—is something hardly anyone I am going to call on wants, until I get there. I know that the many *no's* I may receive may make me feel and act depressed if I let them get the better of me. I know that in order to succeed as a salesman, I have to be continuously on the alert to appear in the right frame of mind. My attitude toward people has to be friendly and cheerful. Regardless of how unlucky I may have been on my earlier calls, I can never reveal that I feel depressed. I must hide all disappointments.

Why is it that people do not look for life insurance and reject, if they can, the life insurance salesman? I can only assume that life insurance is not very important when a man feels happy and healthy. Who wants to die? Even the man who survives a recent cancer operation has no desire to die, and rightfully feels that, regardless of the statistics, he will be the one to live to a ripe old age.

I know from expericnce that I have *to think positively and be enthusiastic at all times.* I have to train myself to stay happy and cheerful. I have to eliminate from my mind *all negative thoughts.* I must like all people. I cannot have any prejudices.

A loving attitude toward all people with the desire to be of service regardless of reward will be one of my most important tools.

If I am not willing to carry this tool with me, I might just as well stay home.

This cannot be emphasized enough.

Now my mind is in the proper frame. I am ready to go. I know that in an honest eight-hour day I will make my quota, which is, as always, A SALE A DAY.

My destination is the Menlo House Restaurant. I am going to meet Mr. Hal Young. *I called him Friday to remind him of our appointment*, which I made with him the previous Tuesday.

151

Experience has taught me that many people will forget something of little importance, such as meeting a life insurance salesman, it is not intentional but it does not have the strength of thought that would accompany something they really wanted.

I arrive at the Menlo House at 7:40 AM. My prospect will meet me at 7:45 AM, I hope. I pick a table in a quiet corner. It is important to arrange for the proper setting. Every little thing is important if I want to do things best. I can watch the entrance. I am seated so that Mr. Young can sit to my right, which is the most effective way for me. I look at my watch: 7:50 AM, 7:55 AM. Will he come? Yes, there is a man at the door. I get up and greet Mr. Young. I introduce myself. We have met only over the phone. But I saw his picture in the business section of our morning paper. Young got a promotion to vice president of his firm. I can tell that his age is about 40. I can guess that his income is in a range to make him an average prospect for me. The article gave his name, residence and family status. He is an ideal prospect.

When I cut his picture from the paper, I knew that many other salesmen would consider him the same way I did. When I called him cold, I used the approach described in chapter 61. I made up the usual prospect card for him. And once I have invested the energy into making up a prospect card, I have to follow through with the effort of *transforming this prospect into a client.* Other salesmen will probably have failed to do so; perhaps I can pick up where they left off. They have energized him with seeds of desire for our product. He will buy some day. Why not from me? And why not right now? But now I have to sell myself to him.

Then I follow the pattern of selling as shown in the form, "Ignoring a Subject or a Problem Won't Solve It." Nothing can demonstrate the need or create the desire for life insurance better in as short a period of time. My associate, Larry Jensen, describes it well in his living trust concept, which is reprinted here with his permission. (See Chapter 60 for Larry Jensen's talk.)

My next call:

It is now 9:30 AM. Mr. Young has left. One prospect's name has been on my mind for a long time. A number of telephone calls to make an appointment with him have failed. I could never get through his secretary but I sensed a good

IGNORING A SUBJECT OR A PROBLEM . . . . WON'T SOLVE IT:

CONFIDENTIAL

My Name_____Birthdate_____

Occupation_____Do I own an interest in the business?_____

My Most Important Assets, Money Can't Buy – My Family:

Wife's Name_____ Birthdate_____ Insured For $_____

Children:_____

My Most Important Asset, Besides My Family, Is My Earning Power:

My net spendable income from my profession or business is: $_____

Continuable Spendable Income from invested capital:

    Real Estate: Market Value $_____ Equity $_____ Income $_____

    Sec. & Bonds: Market Value $_____ Equity $_____ Income $_____

    Cash Savings: Market Value $_____   Income $_____

PRESENT TOTAL SPENDABLE INCOME $_____

From it, I need for myself: (Taxes, Entertainment, Food, Clothes, etc.) $_____

This is the income my family needs without me: $_____

My life insurance will become cash when I die: (Amount) $_____

From that they should set aside for College & Collectable Debts $_____

The net capital left for my family to invest $_____

What is a good return on money (family capital) for a widow
(Net after taxes) @_____% on $_____ is $_____

My Family will have to live on the following income: $_____

My Family needs: $_____

My Family will be short the following income: $_____

At the same rate of interest, it takes $_____ @_____% to provide $_____

These needs and desires do not consider future inflationary trends

Do you know of any commodity or any device by which you can create this principal sum of $_____
simply with the stroke of a pen?

EITHER YOU LET ME TAKE THIS PROBLEM WITH ME OR YOU PUT YOUR FAMILY IN THE
INSURANCE BUSINESS.

6—31—1—65

153

prospect. Should I now throw his card away or make a cold call?

I pass by his building practically every day, but I always have had some excuse not to stop. Why get rejected? Well, this morning I am at least going to make the attempt that will establish him either as a future prospect or as a client, preferably the latter. If I cannot get an appointment, I can always console myself with the fact that most likely others have failed with him as well.

Here is what I say to myself:

He will need life insurance. Everyone does. I am selling a monopoly. We in the life insurance business have no competition. There is no substitute for life insurance. He who does not buy life insurance puts his family or his business into the life insurance business.

I decide to make the phone call, just to check if Mr. Andrew is in. Yes, he is in and I am on my way to make my second call of the day.

I did not wait for the operator to connect me with Mr. Andrew or his secretary. I am going to see him in person.

60—Everybody Is A Manager Of A Large Trust Fund

From Larry Jensen comes this sales idea:

"Mr. Prospect, many people would feel they had financially arrived if they had a trust fund working for them, wouldn't they? Do you know that you have a trust working for you right now? We call it your living trust because it is the value of your expected earning power before your retirement, or, in a trust concept, it's your projected lifetime income.

"Look at it this way. Considering your present yearly salary, you should earn at least another $500,000 by retirement age. It's impossible, of course, for you to lay your hands on that total amount of money all at once. But what you can count on is your salary month after month, year after year, as long as you live.

"Now we look at your salary as interest derived from a trust; in this case, your one-half million dollar living trust. And, as you know, today it is this 'annual interest payment,' if we may call it that, that provides the fine things of life: your warm home; the wonderful happiness you feel as you educate your children; the pride in your wife's appearance; and the respect and pride you have in yourself. Without income, all of this could be lost, couldn't it?

"Mr. Prospect, if you had died yesterday, your magnificent living trust would have died with you. Neither you nor your fine family, for whom you are now working so hard, would realize the peace of mind and security of this one-half million dollars. Now can you say there is not a remote possibility you could have closed your eyes yesterday? Now? Tomorrow? Mr. Prospect, you would fight like a wounded tiger if somebody tried to take away your money or your family security, wouldn't you? The wise family spends considerable effort in protecting its money from needless loss, doesn't it? Mr. Prospect, that is why I am here—to help you protect the income from your most valuable asset, your living trust, against its greatest hazard, your premature death. Wouldn't it be tragic if the one-half million dollars that you will eventually provide for your family were to be lost tonight?

"Fortunately, you can protect against this potential loss. Here is how it works. For a modest 1.5% to 5% carrying charge, my company would step into your shoes, if you stepped out of them, and provide all of the wonderful and anticipated benefits of your living trust to your family. This would be true even if my company received only one carrying charge payment and then you closed your eyes.

"Mr. Prospect, you make about $20,000 a year now. If you were taken out of the picture, how much of your income would continue for your family?" (Let prospect answer). "How much of your income would come from investments? How much would come from real estate? How much of this income would be net after taxes? What do you consider is a good return on money?" (Usually he says about 5%, then you say:) "If you want your family to have 50% of your present income of $20,000, you would need a sum of $200,000 at 5% to produce $10,000 a year before income taxes. What are the amounts you get per year from income producing assets?"

Prospect: "$5,000 a year."

"Therefore, you would need another $100,000 at 5% to produce the other $5,000 per year, wouldn't you? Do you know of any place where we can create this $100,000 at once? Do you know of anybody who would put this up for your family if you were taken out of the picture? Would you like me to establish an account like this for you?"

Try the living trust idea and double your sales.

61—My Telephone Approach To Sell Medical Or Appointment—To Newspaper Leads:

It is best to vary the approach depending on the reaction you get. Your prospect is someone who has had a promotion recently whose name you picked out of the newspaper. Here is an example of a man who, let's say, is with IBM and has become sales manager. Here is what I might say:

"Good morning, Mr. Jones, this is Karl Bach of San Francisco Life Insurance Company. Do you have half a moment? I am calling you because you are a very busy man and you undoubtedly do not want to waste a lot of time with life insurance salesmen. You might even have someone among your friends who is in the life insurance business and, furthermore, you might not wish to spend additional money for life insurance. But, because you are such a busy man and I know you have an open mind—you do have an open mind, don't you? (I WAIT FOR AN ANSWER) I would like to have you measured for your life expectancy. This will enable me to show you a new plan which, if you can qualify, could well double your present life insurance. In some cases this can be done without an additional cash outlay. Is there any reason why you feel you could not qualify?"

You will get all kinds of objections. But if you follow along the above lines most of the time you will get a good reaction. Then you proceed:

"Here is what I would like to do, Mr. Jones. My medical examiner is making a visit in your area this evening and I also have someone being examined in your area tomorrow morning. Now, what would you prefer—morning or evening? I want you to know that this examination is without any obligation on your part as well as on our part; the doctor is on our payroll anyway. It will take about four to six weeks for me to sell you to the insurance company. At that time I will call you and I would like to have you come to my office, or meet me for breakfast or lunch, so that I can show you what I have in mind."

Use applicable free energy questions to disturb and probe and create desire to see you. If you can't sell the medical, then compromise and sell the appointment. Try for your office first, then again compromise to see him at his. Shoot for breakfast or lunchtime appointment.

Remember: "Busy men put their own affairs last."

62—Cold Canvass Doesn't Need To Be Cold

The Case Of Harry Jackson:

Cold canvassing can be one of the most rewarding and enjoyable of experiences for any salesman. Many of my most valuable clients have been found by cold canvassing. Although I do not do much of it today, I often get the urge to call on someone "plain cold," to test my skills in developing business that is sitting there for the asking.

I could probably fill a book on the many outstanding experiences that I have had and about the wonderful people I have met this way. To illustrate a point I would like to tell you about the case of Harry Jackson.

I was giving a talk to a group of life insurance salesmen across the bay in Oakland. The talk was at a morning agency meeting attended by about thirty agents. As I came out of the elevator in the office building where this agency was located, I could not help noticing the big office of a very prominent stockbrokerage firm. The name of the manager, Harry Jackson, was on the door and I found myself wondering if any of the colleagues I was about to address were acquainted with him.

After my talk I started to leave the building, but the urge to find out from Mr. Jackson if anyone had ever called on him was too great. I walked into his office. The receptionist led me to his office. I introduced myself and said:

"Mr. Jackson, my name is Karl Bach and I am in the life insurance business. My office is in San Francisco but I have many prominent clients in Oakland. I just gave a talk to thirty salesmen at the insurance agency down the hall and was just wondering if any of the salesmen had come in to tell you about a new and unusual product designed for men in just your position."

As I had suspected, although Mr. Jackson had been in his office building for five years, no one had made an attempt to meet him or offer him the life insurance he needed so badly. I had the privilege of following his career and increasing his coverage continuously; although it has now been ten years since I first met Harry Jackson, he probably will be purchasing even more life insurance from me in the future. He also has referred me to many outstanding clients.

To me "cold canvassing is gold canvassing." It is an inexhaustible mine and an outstanding vehicle for sharpening a salesman's wits.

The Case Of The Restaurant Owner:

I will never forget the sale I made to Mr. Johnson in my early days when I was calling on restaurant owners on a cold canvass basis. Mr. Johnson bought the largest policy I had ever sold up to that time. The premium was extremely high. In fact, I could not imagine that anyone could earn enough money to pay such a large premium. I was elated with the sale; in fact, everyone in the office, particularly our general agent, was thrilled also.

Three months after the sale, I saw Mr. Johnson on the street. He said, "Karl, I am so grateful for the help you gave me in purchasing my life insurance policy and I like it so very much that I purchased another one just like it from a John Hancock man who called on me the other day."

I never would have believed in a hundred years that such a thing could happen. This lesson has been a most rewarding one for me. As a result, I have made it a habit to call on every one of my new clients, either on the telephone or in person, at least every six months following a sale. If a client relationship has already been built, you can get all the other gentlemen who are trying to energize your client out of the field. Through this method of calling back, I pick up additional business which otherwise would be lost to me.

If I have no breakfast, luncheon or other appointment with a prospect, I make it a point to call on one of my established clients who has purchased all the life insurance he probably will ever buy. My sole purpose on such calls is not to talk about a new purchase. It is often in interviews of this nature that some of my largest sales are created because many of these clients refer me to people they know. Such referrals are on a completely voluntary basis. Also, even though I never bring up the subject of insurance in visits of this type, these clients will frequently ask me about some financial problem that I have overlooked where life insurance is the sole solution.

Since selling is communicating with people, an important lesson that I have learned is that by spending as much time face to face in interviews with prospects, or people who are friendly to us but not prospects, we can improve and build our business to unbelievable heights. The only sin a salesman commits is not making the call. I cannot help comparing this with the farmer. If the farmer did not plow the fields and plant the seeds, he would not be able to harvest. Surely, God created everything on this earth, but he left it up to us to put our intelligence and our energies to work in our chosen fields.

63—What To Do After The Interview

After leaving a client I try to write a memorandum of interview for my files explaining what happened, taking note of various points of information that are essential to the sale. This memorandum is written as a sales document so that when I return to the prospect a second time, it can be used to refresh his memory. That is the most important function of the memorandum of interview, besides its value in future interviews.

The following memoranda are actual cases that resulted in very sizable sales and in building business with some wonderful clients. The case of Dr. Jefferson is one that has repeated itself in similar fashion many times.

On the first interview, at dinner with him, I could not get a decision. It was very difficult to get close to him and to get his confidence. He was still very young and had just started out as an associate of a client of mine, an outstanding orthopedic surgeon. However, he did agree to the medical examination and when his case was approved, I used a memorandum of interview by having him read it. I opened up like this:

"Dr. Jefferson, in order not to waste your valuable time, I thought it best that you read this discussion we had a short time ago. I would like to have your opinion if this isn't exactly what we discussed or if you have any objections to my observations."

Dr. Jefferson had no objections but I could not place the entire amount of insurance that I had recommended. As a general rule, I always try to go high, because it is always easier to settle for less than it is to go up.

On my third interview, which was a breakfast appointment, he went along and the total amount of insurance that I recommended, including an adequate non-cancellable disability income program, was accepted.

The next possible sale for Dr. Jefferson will be insurance on his wife. There is also an inheritance expected in the family and there will be a sizable amount of partnership insurance necessary. I got some hesitation on that action at this time because the doctors are considering incorporating their practice.

First Interview: Summary Of Dinner Discussion With Dr. Jefferson

Following is a summary of ideas discussed with Dr. Jefferson on the subject of his family financial planning. The doctor's family budget at this time is as follows: monthly rent—$375; household help—$200; car expenses—$75; food and miscellaneous—$500; for a total of $1,150 per month or $13,800 per year.

From this $13,800 Dr. Jefferson feels he uses about $2,000 for himself, so that if he were taken out of the picture, his family would need at least $10,000 per year. His present life insurance could be used to provide the education for his children. Additional cash would be needed to purchase a home and provide for other capital expenditures. To provide his family with this needed annual income of $10,000 the capital sum of $200,000 would be required, if Mrs. Jefferson could get a net yield of 5% after income taxes. The premiums which would provide his family with this additional $200,000 insurance estate will not create any financial hardship for Dr. Jefferson at this time. Dr. Jefferson gave me the impression that he believes in term insurance. He is also of the opinion that we will be seeing further inflation in the economy.

I explained our special term plan to Dr. Jefferson. It contains an unusual provision: (1) a special disability waiver clause providing him with the option to have the insurance company continue his protection on a permanent basis for as long as he lives should he become disabled; and (2) a build up of yearly cash value during that period of time. I recommended that we review his program on a yearly basis to adjust it to changing circumstances.

The beneficiary arrangement for his life insurance should be coordinated with an up-to-date will. Because the largest part of his estate at this time would come from life insurance proceeds, he should consider the establishment of a life insurance trust together with a modern will. The services of an attorney specializing in this field are essential. If he doesn't have an attorney, we can recommend several men who have done an outstanding job for many of our clients in this area.

We also discussed the advisability of insuring for an adequate income should he become ill or hurt. The plan I recommend is non-cancellable and guaranteed renewable. The premiums cannot be increased by the insurance company nor can the coverage be changed or exclusions added later. The term "disability" is defined as his inability to *perform his own occupation.* It is payable for his lifetime if disability is caused by an accident and for a five-year period for any one sickness; longer periods are available at higher premiums.

He could have a variation of waiting periods, depending on the premium. For a premium of $28 monthly, we can provide him with an income of $600 per month. It is my feeling that, for the present, a 30-day waiting period would do. I feel that he should consider at least $1,000 per month in the event of sickness or accident.

Having provided an adequate estate for himself and his family in the event of his premature death and an adequate income should he become disabled, he will still have excess funds available for investments. Since he has his entire professional career ahead of him, he will have plenty of time to build a sound investment program for retirement.

Just as it is advisable, if he becomes ill, to get the proper attention by the most competent advisor, it is equally important—when it comes to investments—to seek the guidance of a qualified investment counsellor (not a stockbroker). While it is true that a competent insurance advisor, without a doubt, is most essential when the need for protection is present; he is also important for the maintenance of the proper protection during vacations, periods of disability, and other unusual and unforeseen situations.

On our next interview I will discuss in detail his present life insurance. We will prepare for him our unique Policy Performance Chart (Survey of Life Insurance Estate of) which will include the added protection needed to cover his current objectives.

Second Interview: Summary of Discussion with Dr. Jefferson

We covered the highlights of our last get-together and then reviewed all the doctor's policies. Dr. Jefferson was very much impressed with our policy performance chart because it gave him all the important details pertaining to his life insurance on one page.

We again discussed the importance of proper financial planning and the creation of a life insurance trust together with a will. Dr. Jefferson has become friendly with a competent attorney who will take care of these important details. He went into the pro's and con's of the Keogh plan. We also covered some investment possibilities. Since any investment would take a lot of Dr. Jefferson's time, he felt (and I agreed with him) that mutual funds would be best suited for him at this time.

We discussed the advisability of trading in his present term coverage for permanent life insurance as soon as possible. The following results would be obtained: no decrease in the amount of protection; rates would be the same forever; a guaranteed annual build-up in cash reserves which he should consider as part of his overall investment planning, and which would be available on demand in the future when investment opportunities arise or when cash is needed for some other purpose.

Third Interview: Breakfast Appointment With Dr. Jefferson

I reviewed Dr. Jefferson's financial progress since our last interview and covered a variety of subjects. Dr. Jefferson now owns personal life insurance consisting of $110,000 of non-decreasing insurance and a $41,000 decreasing term contract. Should he pass away at this time, this $151,000 of coverage would provide Mrs. Jefferson with an annual income of approximately $7,500 per year, if she can earn a net rate of 5% after income taxes.

Dr. Jefferson felt that he should add another $100,000 of low premium decreasing term coverage to increase his family

San Francisco Life Insurance Company

SURVEY OF LIFE INSURANCE ESTATE OF _____   BORN _____

	POLICY NO. 1	POLICY NO. 2	POLICY NO. 3	POLICY NO. 4	POLICY NO. 5	POLICY NO. 6	POLICY NO. 7	TOTALS
COMPANY AND POLICY NO.								
ISSUE DATE								
AGE AT ISSUE								
AMOUNT OF INSURANCE	$							
AMOUNT OF TERM RIDERS	$							
KIND OF POLICY								
GUARANTEED RATE OR PAR.								
TOTAL ANNUAL PREMIUM	$							
HOW PAYABLE? M., Q., SA., A.								
DIVIDENDS: HOW APPLIED								
DIVIDEND CASH VALUE								
ADDITIONAL BENEFITS:								
DISABILITY MONTHLY INCOME								
WAIVER OF PREMIUM								
DOUBLE INDEMNITY-ACC.DEATH								
BENEFICIARY								
CONTINGENTS								
OWNERSHIP RIGHTS								
CASH VALUES OF POLICY-NOW	$							
CASH VALUES-NEXT YEAR	$							
CASH VALUES-	$							
CASH VALUES-	$							
PAID-UP VALUES-NOW	$							
AMOUNT OF LOAN	$							
FREE EXTRAS:								
A.P.L.								
C.D.P.								
S.C.P.								
COMMENTS:								

DATE _____   PREPARED BY _____

163

income to $12,500 per year. I recommended a special term plan which decreases at certain intervals and allows for conversion of the decrease regardless of health. This is better than the usual disappearing decreasing term type. The premium for such a policy comes to only $30 per month. The coverage stays level in the amount of $100,000 for the next 2 years and at $80,000 for the following 3 years with an option to exchange the $20,000, which drops off, for permanent life insurance, without medical examination.

We also briefly talked about the advisability of additional disability income. The present coverage provides him with only $600 per month and it is my considered opinion that we should at least double that or provide up to $1500 per month for sickness or accident. Our medical examiner, Dr. Robert Holzman, will complete the necessary forms to see if he can obtain this coverage at this time.

We talked briefly about what to do to save income taxes. Dr. Jefferson's income during the previous year came to $50,000, which puts him in a very nice top tax bracket. Again I recommended that Dr. Jefferson plan for some short term trusts for his children as soon as possible. As far as his investment objectives are concerned, I told him that mine have always been a return *of* money rather than a return *on* the money. I felt that any investments that would take his time would be costly from that point of view. Dr. Jefferson's time is best spent in medicine. Tax advantages alone should never be the sole criterion in making an investment decision. The services of a good investment counsellor should be worth considering. Or Dr. Jefferson should save as much as he can in well-managed mutual funds with growth objectives.

Another important item to consider for Dr. Jefferson is the possibility of incorporating the partnership. This would enable the corporation to have a retirement plan that would create sizable tax deductions way beyond what is possible under the Keogh plan. We will cover this in detail in our next get-together.

Interview With Mr. Max Snell:

I am quite impressed with his beautiful new home and the elegant way it is furnished. It is quite outstanding.

At this time, Max has a gross income of $18,000 per year and Shirley is working to earn the money necessary for Nancy's college fund—she earns $7,000 a year as a legal secretary. Their home has a mortgage of $28,000 and they have paid $19,000 down. It seems to me that their home will have a much greater value in a very short period of time. The monthly payment is $177 plus $100 for taxes.

In my discussion with Max, I tried to develop in my mind what would be most beneficial for the whole family. I tried to put myself in Shirley's place, if something should happen to Max. The following income producing assets would be available in this event:

Group insurance: $25,000

Individual policies: $20,000

Total: $45,000

If this money were put to work at the net rate of 5% per year, Shirley would have slightly over $2,000 per year and that is not considering any unexpected cash demands which could reduce this $45,000. Max mentioned that Shirley would probably sell the house, but even if she did, she would probably have to pay as much in rent, or perhaps slightly less than the payments on the house; so this would not improve her situation very much.

It would be certain that Shirley would have to continue to work regardless of whether she wanted to or was able to. It is for this reason that I personally feel that some additional protection should be added to assure her the privilege of deciding whether or not she would want to work.

We also discussed the time when Shirley and Max will reach retirement age. Here is what we find: there would be approximately $300 per month coming in from Social Security. Life insurance policies will probably provide an income of about $75 per month should Max elect income for life instead of cash. The retirement plan with his company should provide Max with an income of $500 per month for life. He was not certain about this. Therefore, at age 65 Max and Shirley would both have approximately $900 per month coming in.

By that time their home will be paid for and the children will be self-supporting so the income situation at retirement doesn't look very bad. Max will have the opportunity beginning

January 1st to start an investment program in which his company adds 50% to every dollar he puts in. I advised him to take advantage of that opportunity. Because of this, Max's desire for other investments was not quite as urgent as the desire to provide extra protection in the form of income for Shirley.

I recommended to Max that we purchase $20,000 of permanent life insurance to put Shirley in a more independent position. This would also provide in itself an extra income benefit of $90 per month at retirement age with an option to increase it to $300 per month by adding additional cash at age 65, which could come from the investment fund with his employer. Assuming that Max does not make any other investments, he then would enjoy an income of over $1,200 per month at retirement age. In the meantime this extra $20,000 life insurance would provide additional cash reserves.

Since Max's medical examination qualified him for the lowest rate, his cash at age 65 will be greater than the premiums paid in. I recommended waiver of premium which guarantees completion of the plan should Max become disabled. I also suggested that he consider adding an additional protection rider with an option to increase deposits at a later date, because when Nancy has finished college there will be additional cash available for investments.

I suggested that Max put a binder on the protection but he felt he wanted to think it over. And knowing him to be responsible and reliable, I know that he will. I am holding Max's check until November 30. Unless I hear from Max before this date we will put $20,000 of permanent life insurance in force. I will also ask the underwriter to grant me permission to add an additional $30,000 protection rider before December 30, without an additional health examination.

If Max follows my advice, I am convinced that he will be building a sounder financial foundation. His overall planning will be balanced and he cannot make a mistake, whether he dies too soon or lives too long.

How To Handle The Memorandum of Interview With Business Insurance Prospects

The memorandum of interview with Mr. Sam Smith, president of the Smith-Jones Corporation, is designed to demonstrate the real need for business life insurance. It does not cover any technical details but clearly demonstrates the need for additional life insurance on Sam and on his key man. Sam Smith was originally brought to my attention when his picture appeared in the newspaper as having started the Smith-Jones Corporation. To date, this firm has purchased several million dollars worth of life insurance from me and when Fred Jones left Smith-Jones Corporation, he started another company which today is also one of my most important clients.

The memorandum of interview with the two principals of Export International resulted in one of my largest cases. Here the interview was tough and the clients said very little, not even *yes* to my proposition. Once they had read the memorandum (I mailed it to them unsolicited) they called me and asked me to work with their attorney.

Memorandum Of Interview With Mr. Sam Smith:

Sam told me of the change in the company. Since my last visit, Sam-Fred Corporation had bought out Fred Cook, a co-founder. Sam had to co-sign a note for a large bank loan to effect the purchase. For this reason, the personal affairs of Sam Smith had to be reviewed with a different objective in mind. Sam now owned in excess of 70% of the company—which is his biggest personal asset. The other assets owned by him are primarily his home and his personal property.

I pointed out to Sam that he is like many of my close corporation clients who are building businesses and putting all their efforts and earnings back into the business. Because of our present tax structure, they retain all profits and do not pay out dividends. This is good for the owner, but not practical for the family of the owner should he die prematurely.

In Sam's case, there would be a large estate tax and substantial probate charges to be paid by his wife at his death. The creditors of the company would be taken care of first in addition to the large bank loan which is insured and was made in connection with the purchase of the stock of Mr. Cook. The problem that Sam's family would be facing would be the continuation of income and, naturally, the disposition of the business. Should it be continued, the family could control it or it could be sold with the money reinvested by Mrs. Smith to provide income. Another factor that I considered and discussed with Sam was the probability of his son coming into his business. Richard is now 16 years of age and it is not in the too distant future that this could be a great possibility.

I suggested that the company consider an employment contract with Sam which would provide a continuation of a certain percentage of his present income for his family, for a certain number of years after his death. This compensation agreement could be funded with a low premium life insurance policy. At death, the insurance would bring tax free money into the corporation, which then could afford to pay Mrs. Smith an annual income of, say, $12,000 for ten years without reduction in surplus. In fact, the insurance would create a continuous surplus even after this ten-year period because the $12,000 paid to Mrs. Smith would be tax deductible by the corporation. With such a plan, Mrs. Smith would not be forced to look for liquidation or for a buyer of the business or immediate action should something happen to Sam.

The company owns only a $50,000 policy on Mark Fisher, a valuable key man; I also recommend additional coverage on his life. Mr. Smith is considering this suggestion. A deferred compensation plan would also be advisable for Mark Fisher. According to Sam, Mark now owns about 24% of the stock of the company and several other key men in the firm own the remaining 6%.

I consider it of great importance that at some later date a deferred compensation arrangement for all key men be studied. Such a deferred compensation arrangement when it is properly funded with life insurance would be profitable to the company in the long run. The company has to make a profit, simply because it, as a corporation, does not die and the key men do. Also, as long as the present tax law does not require the taxing of the proceeds of life insurance, the corporation cannot afford to be without it.

I discussed with Mr. Smith the pros and cons of making his personal life insurance proceeds payable to a trust. We also covered the advantages and disadvantages of various ownership arrangements. We discussed the advisability of looking into the creation of a short term trust for Sam's three children. I promised Sam that I would discuss it with George Rogers, his attorney.

Sam agreed to a mortality study (medical exam) for himself and Mark. Dr. Holzman will see them in two days at 9:00 AM.

168

Memorandum Of Interview With Messrs. Henry Morris and David Clark:

During the interview I discovered that the present value of Export International could be stated very modestly at $1,000,000. I explained to Henry and David that their present arrangements should be reviewed, particularly their stock retirement agreement, to make certain there is no hardship should either of them pass away.

Another problem that they should consider solving is the matter of income for their wives. I recommended an employment contract giving the wives an income after death of, say, $10,000 per year for ten years (deferred compensation). Thus, the corporation which now does not pay dividends, would be able to pay the widows an income. It could be funded with life insurance and would always create a profit for the corporation because the income was deductible. I also suggested that it would not be a bad idea to consider putting the wives on a salary now. Thus they could become participants in the pension and profit sharing plan with all the fringe benefits connected therewith.

I had made a study of their present pension and profit sharing trust agreement which is excellent. It gives Henry and David the opportunity to have the pension and profit sharing plan purchase life insurance on their lives with funds from the pension and profit sharing plan. This would make funds available if death should occur to either: have the plan buy stock in Export International, if it is permissible at the time, or with the proper collateral, the trustees could probably lend the survivors money to purchase the stock of the deceased.

We discussed the differences in cost of life insurance for Henry and David who both qualified as excellent risks on their last examinations. Because of the high cost of money, I recommended, that for the next two years, we have the corporation purchase term insurance, because of the low cash outlay, but with an option to convert retroactively with a recoupment of premiums at the end of two years or before.

I am holding a check in my file as a binder for $100,000 each on Henry and David. Either Henry or David will call me before next Wednesday in the event that they should change their minds as to the binder.

Neither Henry nor David had very much personal life insurance to cover the death tax liabilities created by the size of his present estate. Like most men who are building up corporations, they are plowing most of their earnings back into Export International, and rightly so.

The largest family asset is the stock of Export International. Since a widow normally would not invest in such a closed corporation, all of the above-mentioned ideas deserved very careful consideration, as it is always better to prevent problems than to realize that they might exist sometime and do nothing.

Henry and David will both see doctors for their electrocardiograms and X-rays to determine if they can qualify for additional life insurance, in order to bring that phase of their financial picture in line with their current status. By transferring the risk to an insurance company, they are in a better position to face the future. It seems that future growth is probably going to magnify all of these problems which are present ones, however, so that any insurance that they purchase today probably will not remain sufficient. However, some coverage, even if inadequate, is better than no coverage at all.

It would be advisable for me to consider studying Henry's and David's personal estate situations on an individual basis in the not too distant future. I should recommend to them to consider the uses of a modern living trust with a pour-over provision in their wills which can save them from many problems.

Henry told me that he has been quite busy due to Charlie Carter's trip to the Orient. He felt that Charlie was a key man and I recommended that we get him examined the following Wednesday by Dr. Holzman to see if he can qualify for key man life insurance. There certainly would be an economic loss to Export International should Charlie die. It is not easy today to get people with the experience and background necessary to do his job. There is no sense in Henry and David making life tougher when they can make it easier for themselves.

This key man coverage probably should be purchased by Export International. But it certainly would be advisable to have some coverage of this type also in the pension and profit sharing plan, because profits are made by key men.

170

64—The Proper Use Of The Medical Examination

The medical examiner can be as helpful an ally and partner as a life insurance man ever can expect. I believe that if it were not for the help of the many outstanding physicians who have made examinations for me over the years, I never would have accomplished what I have in the life insurance business. Because of the importance of the medical examiner, I have dedicated this chapter to him.

I could mention many examiners with whom I have worked over 20 years and to whom I am very grateful. Many of them have helped build their practices by meeting my clients through insurance examinations.

The other day one of my associates told me about a million dollar case that he had lost. When I delved into the details of why he had lost the case, I discovered that one reason was that he had mishandled the medical examination. His prospect was willing to take the examination, but the agent decided to let the nurse of a doctor he did not know arrange for the appointment. The agent's reason was that that particular doctor's office was close to his prospect's office. Since he had no knowledge of the reliability of the doctor or his staff, the agent was relying on an unknown quantity in an examination for a million dollar case.

The agent did know that an appointment had been set up for two examinations and an electrocardiogram. But later the doctor's office cancelled the appointment without informing the agent of its action. When he found out, it was too late. The prospect had gone on a business trip and when he returned, he had changed his mind about making another appointment.

To me, setting up the medical examination is the most important part of the selling process. I would never rely on a strange doctor to set up an appointment; nor would I even rely on my own well-qualified secretary, unless I know both my client and the doctor very, very well.

I had to learn this the hard way over a period of many years. It would behoove every agent to pay close attention to setting up the proper appointment at the proper time and under the most desirable circumstances. In many instances when I am not certain in my own mind that the prospect will keep his appointment, I arrange to pick him up personally to take him to the doctor's office. In other instances when I am not sure that the prospect will go on his own to the doctor's office, and I do not want to waste my own time, I have a doctor available who has proved his reliability over a long period of time. I set up an appointment for the doctor to visit my prospect at his office or home.

My doctors know that if the prospects do not keep appointments or if the clients keep them waiting, I will reimburse them for their valuable time. I respect my doctor's time and, in return, they respect mine.

Furthermore, I like a doctor who will give my prospect a thorough physical examination because I do not like for a prospect to feel he has qualified too easily. It is much better if the insurance I would like to have him purchase seems more difficult to obtain than he had realized. A person wants something that is hard to get that much more. Therefore, don't use doctors who do not give good physical examinations.

Over the years I had to learn a lot about the doctors themselves. I am thinking in particular of one physician, who in his early years of performing our examinations, was outstanding but who after becoming busy was not interested in life insurance examinations. As a consequence, I had to pay a price because although he promised to do so, he did not make exams he previously would have. He had become unreliable but this only became apparent to me after the passage of some time.

One has to take a particular interest in the personality of the doctor as it appears to the prospect. Where women are concerned, you do not want to use a very young doctor but you do want one whose personality is pleasing. Men are not so particular. However, the attitude of the examiner frequently will have a direct bearing on those cases too.

There is no end to the problems a life insurance agent encounters before he cements a life insurance sale, but the more attention he pays to the details of the medical examination—the time, the place and the circumstances—the greater his results will be.

Points On The Proper Use Of The Medical Examination

On Women:

Women should go to the doctor's office. It might be wise for you to emphasize that no pelvic examination is involved. As a rule, women avoid medical examinations unless reassured that there is no pelvic examination necessary.

Points To Remember:

The doctor has to be reliable. Times set should be convenient to both doctor and client so that there is no rushing. The place should be proper and convenient for both doctor and client. Dates should not be set too far ahead. I like it best if it's no longer than three days. Times are generally best if the examination is at the client's office before his staff arrives. If at the client's home, the best time is the weekend. It is better to avoid home visits because the wife is often irritated and not understanding. Children, animals and TV often interfere. However, each situation is special and an individual deserves your maximum attention. Another reason why it is wise to avoid evenings for the examination is that the prospect is usually tired from working. The client's mood should be as receptive as possible.

Sell the Doctor:

In my own operation I have a special examining room in my office and one of my medical examiners spends the entire day of Wednesday making examinations. Your doctor should be able to take a careful and detailed medical history. This saves a lot of time in clearing the cases with the underwriter.

65—Can There Be Free Energy In A Bad Investment?

Whenever I take the commuter train to my office, I pick a likely prospect to sit with. This is easily accomplished when I walk down the aisle. I can see for myself if a prospect is young or old, poorly or well-dressed, healthy or sickly looking. I have about 45 minutes of traveling time. Not a bad way to get the day started.

I have made many sales this way over the years and have made many friends. Many people are much richer now because I have chosen to sit next to them on the commuter train.

When I sit down next to a stranger, I introduce myself by handing out one of my ballpoint pens which bears the slogan, "I don't sell insurance; I help you buy it." The following incident transpired one morning with a stockbroker.

"Have one of my cards, Sir." I handed him my pen. Usually, the stranger begins to read what is printed on the pen, chuckling at the slogan. I then ask the prospect for his card. The man I was sitting next to that day—I shall call him Mr. Frank—was a partner in one of the city's large stockbrokerage firms.

After he saw that I was in the life insurance business, he said: "Mr. Bach, I want you to know that I am not in the least interested in life insurance. Life insurance is the worst investment a man can make."

I replied: "Mr. Frank, I have to agree with you one hundred per cent. Life insurance should never be a good investment, because if it should become a good investment, it is a bad investment for the insurance company. May I ask you a couple of questions, Mr. Frank? How many times earnings are you selling for?" and I kept quiet.

His answer was: "I have enough insurance."

I then proceeded: "Are you considering yourself a growth or an income stock?" And I said it with a chuckle.

He said: "I never thought of life insurance this way."

A very lively conversation developed. By the time we had reached San Francisco, we had become very well acquainted and I was able to add a new client to my ever-increasing chain of valuable policyholders.

Many times those persons like Mr. Frank, who make the statement, "Life insurance is a bad investment; I am not interested in life insurance," really want to be shown that they are wrong.

"One should never buy life insurance in order to get a good return on one's money. However, one should always keep in mind that life insurance is bought to benefit the beneficiary, not the insured. And certainly, the beneficiary can never get as much return on the investment of the premium as when the life insurance policy becomes a claim."

66—A Special Tribute

This book would not be complete without giving some special tribute and words of appreciation to a man who has probably had the greatest influence on my career—Harry M. Stone, now retired at Sun City, Arizona. Harry came to California many years ago after a long and successful estate planning career in the East. His entire business lifetime had been spent working with life insurance agents as an "architect for their prospects' financial present and for their families' financial future."

To state what Harry has done for me would mean writing an entire new book. However, at my strong and continual suggestion, he will publish his own book in the not too distant future. I hope that every reader will take advantage of this accumulation of knowledge and treasure chest of wisdom when it finally is made available.

What I wish to pass on to the reader here is one important lesson that Harry taught me that I believe everyone can use. When I met Harry over 20 years ago, I was considered very successful in the life insurance business. I was producing $2,000,000 to $3,000,000 per year. In those days that was a lot of production. Harry helped me raise my sights to a million a month, or better.

He pointed out to me that most insurance men were jumping all over the prospect field looking for new clients, while someone else was cultivating their old ones. Why not do the best job you can for the clients you have and save yourself the time of seeking out new prospects before it is necessary? Although he is a technician and master designer of financial blueprints and not a salesman, Harry has tremendous conviction for the role that life insurance plays in the affairs of families and businesses. He instilled in me his strong belief in the financial miracle of life insurance and his deep desire that every client have a complete financial plan properly drafted by competent legal counsel, co-ordinated with all life insurance assets. As life insurance men, we have the unique opportunity of playing the role of an architect for the financial planning which the client so desperately needs and often fails to receive.

I made it a practice to discuss my client's financial affairs with Harry Stone. As a result, on many occasions he pointed out an additional need for life insurance that I had completely overlooked. Harry's deep insight into human nature probably helped him see situations that were hardly visible to anyone else.

There are many life underwriters in the San Francisco Bay Area and in Arizona to whom I have introduced Harry Stone. Their success is living evidence of what he has done for them and for me. If you know Andy Wolff of Flagstaff, Arizona, you might ask him about Harry Stone. If you know Arnold Panella of Daly City, California, you might ask him about Harry Stone. Men such as Robert Ronald, Robert Williams, Carroll Walker, Bob Woodward, Robert Connelly, Robert Goodenough, Arthur Cameron, Gordon Maxson, Bob Nelson, Maurice Edelstein, Don Stutsman, Al Hill, Larry Jensen, Bill Montague—all members of the Million Dollar Round Table—are the beneficiaries of Harry's great mind and his deep conviction.

67—In Conclusion:

I asked myself why I wanted to write this book and I came to the conclusion that everything in life needs selling. The reason I started to write is the fact that several friends had urged me to do just that. Through a very nice method of selling, they put the seeds in my mind to go to work for this work of love. In compiling these pages, I probably have had more fun than any financial remuneration can bring, regardless of how successful this book may be.

I also know that the greatest satisfaction that any man can receive will come if the ideas expressed herein are used by a salesman who wants to do a bigger job (and I have to emphasize "wants"). His increased production will be the greatest reward that I can derive. I know that the salesman who sells more is a happier salesman and when he is happier, his family is happier and his associates are happier. He radiates more happiness than ever before. What greater reward in life can there be than to make other happy?

Selling has given me many wonderful times and great satisfaction. Never in my life have I felt that I was actually working on a job. My days spent in business have always, been too short. There were never enough hours to do all the things that I wanted to do.

If you do not have this joy of accomplishment, I do not believe there is a better way to get it than by studying your business as often and as much as you can; but it should be done off your business hours. And I stress OFF YOUR BUSINESS HOURS.

Too many salesmen are overeducated and underworked. You cannot substitute studying time for calling—on—prospects time. But if you can find the time in which to enrich and perfect your operation, without sacrificing production time, you will improve beyond your wildest dreams. But you have to do it continually and it has to be a never-ending process. If you can enjoy helping people, regardless of what they do for you, this too will help you to grow—not only in business, but as a human being. If you will understand others, they will understand you. But never expect perfection. Never expect Utopia. It can never come. Just as there is rain and snow as well as sunshine, you have to keep in mind that beyond the clouds, the sun is always shining.

68—Now You Have Read This Book—So What?

You probably have read many books on salesmanship and now you have read one more. If you are like most people, you will never put a new idea to work. If you are like most people, you will not change your old habits and you will say to yourself, "What Karl Bach can do, I can never do. I can never be like him. I have my own style and I have to be myself." This is exactly the way I used to feel when I listened to successful salesmen, but I learned by trying and working on new ideas to improve myself.

The reason for someone else's success is generally something that can be explained and can be duplicated. Most ideas are transferable from one person to another. I have also come to the conclusion that since Edison invented the electric light bulb, there is no need to invent it all over again. In other words, learn from other men's experience. We all walk into a dark room and switch on the light. The work to create this miracle was performed by Edison. But we all are getting the benefit of his experience and his many years of drudgery in developing his invention into a useful form.

Therefore, I established early in my career that I would put to work what I can adopt. I will add to my system of selling what others have already experienced and I will start doing it right now. I will make up my mind that perhaps I can do even a little better than I have done up to now, equipped as I am with these ideas that others have developed.

Therefore, reader of this book, why not use some of the notes you took while reading this book and put them to work today? Perhaps you can find one idea that will work for you. If you can put only one new idea into practice, it will be worth your while. But if you care to study this book more closely, you will find new horizons of success you never thought were within your power to reach.

This will be my greatest reward for the labor and effort in writing these pages.

AFTERWORD: TEN CHALLENGES

1. Am I willing to pay the price of success?

2. Am I willing to listen to the ideas of other successful men in order to reach my own goal without repeating mistakes?

3. Am I willing to share my experiences with others in order to make my business a better one for all?

4. Am I willing to work hard and, in the early years, long hours in order to make the later years more secure?

5. Am I willing to do the things that unsuccessful men will not do, the things the successful man will do?

6. Can I operate my business in such a way as to make my industry proud of me? Am I proud of the performance of life insurance and of the value of my product?

7. Do I express my ideas to my prospect in language which he understands? Do I keep my sales talk simple?

8. Do I advise my prospect as I would advise myself in the same position?

9. Am I willing to call in an "expert" before I ruin my chances to close a sale?

10. Do I have the courage to make myself see enough people to give myself a fair chance to succeed in the great business of which I am a part?

Appendix

1. Explanation of the formula "1 + 1 = 1," referred to in chapter 17. The following is an excerpt from the author's book, *How I Sell $12,000,000 of Life Insurance, Year After Year*, (Palo Alto, California; Pacific Books; 1960), pp. 50-51:

One Plus One Equals One

It has been my experience that by working out each step at a time and as though it were a complete entity in itself, I give myself the best possible chance to make a sale. In this way, I keep the whole process at its simplest in my contact with a prospect.

Every interview represents a series of steps. For example, step 1, you must introduce yourself? step 2, introduce your produce; etc. The steps can be adjusted according to the individual interview. I discuss this point in more detail later, but now let's direct our attention to giving yourself a chance.

I treat each step as a complete entity, as though it were a sale in itself. I proceed to the next step only after I feel that previous one is a settled issue.

The idea now is to put that first step out of my mind. It is over and done with. The next step becomes a brand new sale, and so is again represented by the figure one.

Nothing can be considered accomplished until the interview is culminated by a sale. And that final closing is once more represented by the figure one.

Thus, I progress from one to one to one—until I reach the final one. And that is the simple explanation of the somewhat perplexing formula: 1 + 1 = 1.

Let's consider what would happen were I to use a more conventional approach.

I would progress from step one to step two, from step two to step three, and follow in consecutive order. But a *sales interview is not an automatic machine.* A variety of things can arise. The good salesman must anticipate this and be prepared for sudden changes in his tactics. This means the salesman must be sensitive and flexible. I would not be able to predetermine four steps or seven steps. *You cut down you chances* if you think of an interview in terms of a fixed process with a prescribed schedule or structure.

The point I want to emphasize is to take one step at a time in selling. For example, one step might relate to the needs of the prospect. When that is accomplished, I close the door on that aspect, and go on to whatever step is indicated by the developments in the interview. Thus, the prospect, too, is involved in taking but one step at a time, without being confused or overwhelmed by a barrage of ideas. . .

2. Excerpt from page 55 of the author's book (see above) referred to in chapters 20 and 47:

Seven Words That
Can Protect You
from Failure

You may have seen these words in sales literature before, but not, I believe, in the same way I use them.

The first five magic words are: WHO, WHY, WHAT, WHERE, and WHEN.

The sixth and seventh are WOW and HOW. I shall discuss these later, but WOW is the big word here.

I put these words to use constantly. They are fundamental to my selling success.

It is the sequence of these words that is important!

W H O — W H Y — W H A T — W H E R E — WHEN — WOW — HOW.

You give yourself the best chance to sell if you use them in that order. . .